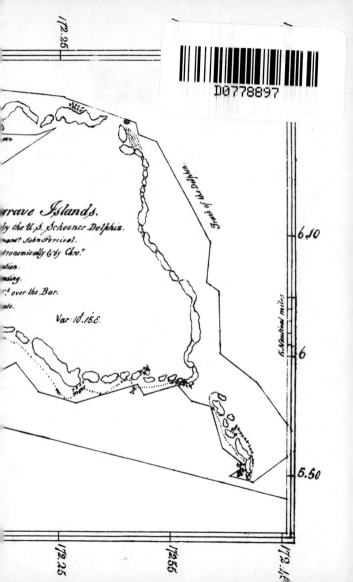

...rave *Islands*.

...by the U.S. Schooner Dolphin.

...mand.* John Percival.

...tronomically & by Chro.*

...tion.

...nding.

...t over the Bar.

...ds.

Var: 10.15.E.

Freak of the Dolphin

172.25

172.55

172.35

6.10

6

5.50

K. Nautical miles

JOURNAL

OF A

CRUISE

OF THE

UNITED STATES SCHOONER DOLPHIN

IN PURSUIT OF THE MUTINEERS OF THE

WHALE SHIP GLOBE

HIRAM PAULDING
Rear-Admiral, U. S. N.
About 1863

JOURNAL

OF A

CRUISE

OF THE

UNITED STATES SCHOONER DOLPHIN

AMONG THE ISLANDS OF THE PACIFIC OCEAN

AND A VISIT TO THE MULGRAVE ISLANDS,

IN PURSUIT OF THE MUTINEERS OF THE WHALE SHIP GLOBE

WITH A MAP

By Lieut. HIRAM PAULDING, of the U.S. Navy

WITH A NEW INTRODUCTION
By A. GROVE DAY,
Senior Professor of English, Emeritus,
University of Hawaii

HONOLULU
UNIVERSITY OF HAWAII PRESS
1970

First published in New York, 1831
New Impression published in 1970 by C. Hurst & Co.,
40a Royal Hill, Greenwich, London S.E.10
and in the United States of America
by the University of Hawaii Press
535 Ward Avenue, Honolulu, Hawaii 96814

Introduction © by A. Grove Day, 1970

SBN 87022-616-9

Library of Congress Catalog Card No. 77-119793

Printed in Great Britain

INTRODUCTION

———

THE cruise of the U.S. Schooner *Dolphin* in 1825 and 1826 ties together several striking themes of Pacific history: whaling, the goriest mutiny in oceanic annals, the beginnings of the United States as a Pacific power, American naval life, early contacts with South Sea peoples, and missionary difficulties in the Sandwich or Hawaiian Islands. It deals with blackest crime and amazing heroism, massacres and Christian congregations. The only account of this cruise is the little book by First Lieutenant Hiram Paulding.

The story of the *Dolphin* begins with the story of the *Globe*. Samuel Comstock, harpooner on the New England whale ship *Globe*, aged twenty-one, at midnight on Sunday, January 25, 1824, near Fanning Island in the equatorial Pacific, with the help of Silas Payne and several other hard cases recruited at Honolulu, led the mutiny. Almost single-handed, Sam murdered all four officers and ordered the horrified crew to sail southward in search of a South Sea island where he could set up a dream kingdom. The island Sam chose was the "Mulgrave Range," better known as Mili Atoll in the Marshall group—a region today comprised in the United States Trust Territory of the Pacific Islands.

Mili lies at the southern tip of the eastern Ratak (Sunrise) chain of the Marshalls, and consists of a group of islets surrounding a lagoon. The inhabitants had known few white men, and Comstock's mad scheme might have worked had he not aroused the suspicions of Payne and the others. They feared he would get the natives to attack the crew. The mutineers fell out among themselves. Comstock was ambushed and murdered, and then the natives massacred most of the remaining crew. Six of the men, however, had managed to cut the cable of the *Globe* and sail blindly eastward. With no instruments except a stolen compass, with no navigator aboard, and with so few hands to manage the vessel, these six made an amazing passage to Valparaiso, Chile, and gave their version of the mutiny to the world.

Opinion was aroused in New England, and eventually orders were sent from Washington to Commodore Isaac Hull in the Pacific. He detached the *Dolphin* on a mission to apprehend the mutineers presumed to remain on Mili, and asked for volunteers for what was to prove a lengthy but exciting cruise.

The *Dolphin* was a fast schooner of 180 tons, 88 feet long and provided with 12 guns. She was commanded by the legend-making John Percival (1779–1862), who had won the sobriquets of "Mad Jack" and "Roaring Jack." He had gone to sea at the age of thirteen "with only nine months' schooling and a clean shirt." Percival had been a master in the Atlantic and West Indies before being "pressed" in 1797 into the British Navy at Lisbon. Reluctantly serving on H.M.S. *Victory* and other ships, after two years he led a group of other Americans in a break for liberty and escaped to a Yankee merchantman. He entered the United States Navy and passed the ranks of master and midshipman. During the War of 1812 he armed a fishing smack and captured a British tender lured close to him off New York. He chased pirates in the West Indies, and in 1823 joined the Pacific Exploring Squadron as first lieutenant of Hull's flagship, the U.S.S. *United States*. "Mad Jack" had a reputation as a fiery and humorsome man but a superb seaman, and was an excellent choice to command a vessel seeking to round up a gang of mutineers.

Percival's first officer, and the author of the *Journal*, was Hiram Paulding (1797–1878), whose father had helped to capture Major John André, hanged as a British spy during the Revolution. Hiram was well educated for his time and was appointed a midshipman in the American Navy in 1811. His gallant services at the Battle of Lake Champlain as acting lieutenant in the *Ticonderoga* were recognized by Congress with the award of $1,500 prize money and a sword. Fighting Barbary pirates in the *Constellation* brought promotion to lieutenant in 1816, and he spent the next three years cruising the Pacific in the *Macedonian*. After graduation from a military academy in Vermont he returned to the Pacific in the *United States*. He was chosen to carry Commodore Hull's dispatches from Callao, Peru, to the mountain headquarters of General Simon Bolivar in the Andes; his journey of

1,500 miles on horseback was later to be narrated in his other book, *Bolivar in His Camp* (New York, 1834). The following year he volunteered to serve under Percival on the *Dolphin* cruise, which was to result in his best-known book.

The schooner sailed from Chorillos in Peru on August 18, 1825, and after obtaining provisions along the coast visited the Galápagos Islands on the equator. There the crew loaded more than a hundred of the giant tortoises that gave the group its Spanish name. These creatures, observed by Charles Darwin and other scientists in later years, were added to the ship's stores, and without being fed lasted alive until after Christmas. At Charles Island (Santa María) they stopped at Essex Bay, named for Commodore David Porter's raider in the War of 1812, and saw the barrel used by whalers as a maritime post office.

Approaching the Marquesas group late in September, the *Dolphin* passed "Rooahooga" (Ouahouka), one of the southernmost islands, and then visited La Dominica (Hiva Oa) and "Nooaheeva" or Nuku Hiva. Paulding gives an account of the valley of Typee or Taipi, inhabited by "the most warlike" of the tribes, where Herman Melville, deserter from a whale ship, was to spend a month among the cannibals sixteen years later. Leaving Taiohae or Comptroller's Bay, the *Dolphin* also stopped at Massachusetts Bay, where Porter had built a fort and claimed Nuku Hiva for the United States in 1813. Paulding's description of the Marquesas at this period, when the islands were inhabited by many handsome, lively people, is in contrast with later sad accounts of this heavily depopulated group.

Departing on October 5 south of Nuku Hiva, with "Rooahooga and Rooapooa" (Ouahouka and Ouapou) in sight, the *Dolphin* sailed for six hundred miles before touching on the 10th at uninhabited Caroline Island, lying on the tenth south parallel. Thence she headed for the Tokelau or Union group. Paulding's descriptions of Duke of Clarence Island (Fakaofo) and Duke of York Island (Atafu) are valuable early accounts.

Byron's Island (Nukunau in the southern Gilberts) was sighted on November 9; it had been discovered by John Byron in the British *Dolphin* in 1765—not, as Paulding's book has it, in 1791. Hiram's account of the warlike Gilbertese, who fought his crew when a musket was stolen and taken ashore, is an enlightening early view of these islanders. The plight of "Roaring Jack" Percival, whose boat smashed on a reef and left him defenseless under a shower of stones, must have made him roar louder than any "savage".

After his rescue, in three or four hours the *Dolphin* made Drummond's Island (Tabiteuea), From there it was a matter of nine days' sailing to reach the crew's goal—the Mulgrave Islands, which they sighted on November 19 and where they hoped to track down the *Globe* mutineers.

Paulding's tale of the search for survivors and his inclusion of the narratives of William Lay and Cyrus Hussey, captives of the Marshallese warriors, are vital parts of the *Globe* episode. Hiram is too modest in his account of the rescue of Lay, in which he, as head of the launch party, took the lead. A midshipman in the launch, Charles Henry Davis, remembered that "the boldest act he ever witnessed" was Paulding's seizure of Lay in the face of a mob of several hundred infuriated tribesmen, armed with clubs and spears. During the parley, Paulding suddenly grabbed the presumed mutineer Lay. Covering his own body with his human prize and holding a cocked pistol to Lay's ear, Hiram marched him to the launch before the Marshallese men could recover from their surprise at Paulding's audacity. The capture of

Lay was the key to the whole aftermath of the *Globe* saga.

The life of the dwellers on Mili is graphically pictured in Paulding's book. He includes the first map of Mili and shows the tracks of the schooner and the launch. He describes the meager diet of breadfruit, "bup" or edible pandanus, and fish caught by the use of a driving method.

The *Dolphin* did not depart from Mili until December 9, when a visit was made to "South Pedder's Island"—probably Maloe-lap. Here the high chief of the group resided, who said that only once had white men visited his island, "in a large vessel" a long time before. Nearby "Ibbitson's Island" was apparently Aur.

At the end of the year the *Dolphin* headed for the Hawaiian chain. They approached "Ballard's Rock" (Gardner Pinnacles) on January 2, 1826, and on the 9th, Captain Percival had another shore adventure when marooned overnight on Bird Island or Nihoa. On the 11th, the vessel skirted "Onehow" (Niihau) and "Atooi" (Kauai), heading for "Wahoo" or Oahu. The schooner rounded the north shore of that island and was not towed into Honolulu Harbor until the 16th.

Paulding's accounts of the Hawaiian or

Sandwich Islands in 1826 are valued supple-
ments to others better known. He not only
went ashore at "Onavoora"—surely among
the most curious of the variant spellings of
Honolulu—but explored the Pearl River
valley, site of the present main American
naval base in the Pacific. He climbed the
fortified Punchbowl Crater. He met the
eleven-year-old King Kamehameha III, the
Queen Regent Kaahumanu, and the "prime
minister" Kalanimoku, who had been nick-
named "Billy Pitt." Hiram chatted with
Chief Boki and his wife Liliha, who had
visited London with the ill-fated party of
King Kamehameha II (Liholiho). Paulding
also enjoyed meeting John Wilkinson, an
Englishman who had come to Hawaii in
Lord Byron's *Blonde*, the ship that returned
the bodies of Liholiho and his queen to
Honolulu. Wilkinson had begun raising crops
in broad Manoa Valley; he was a pioneer in
the sugar industry in the Hawaiian Islands.
Percival used as interpreter Don Francisco
de Paula Marín, called "Manini" by the
Hawaiians, an eccentric Spaniard who had
imported many plants and became the head
physician of old Kamehameha I. The officers
of the *Dolphin* also met Hiram Bingham and
others of the "First Company" of Congrega-

tionalist missionaries, who had brought the
Gospel to the islanders six years earlier.

The *Dolphin* spent more than four months
at Honolulu, refitting and carrying on
business ashore. She was the first American
naval vessel to visit the future Fiftieth State.
Neither the Hawaiians nor the American
missionaries were pleased by the activities of
Captain Percival. "Mad Jack", an ardent
fighting man, was no diplomat. He had been
commissioned by Commodore Hull to see
about the collection of more than $300,000
in debts that the Hawaiian chiefs had run up
as a result of the sales activities of American
merchants. The royal family and the chiefs
had filled their grass shacks with silks,
foreign costumes, imported liquors, blue
willow-ware dinner sets, billiard tables, and
gilded mirrors. They were supposed to pay
in sandalwood, a tree growing in the mountains that yielded a fragrant wood highly
prized in the Orient. Gangs of Hawaiians
were recruited without pay to haul out the
trees from the hills and forests. They looted
almost all the stands, so that the boom was
dying but the businessmen were pressing for
payment. Percival obtained from the chiefs
an acknowledgment that the creditors should
be paid by the government. This was the

origin of one of the Hawaiian kingdom's
most modern trappings—a national debt.

Paulding in his book passes over in a para-
graph an episode still remembered in Hawaii.
Since the day that Captain James Cook
discovered the islands, it had been customary
for women to swim out to arriving ships;
and as one early seafarer remarked, "not
many of the crew proved to be Josephs".
As soon as they could, the missionaries got
the chiefs to pass edicts putting a stop to
this hospitable gesture. The resentment of
some crews was violent. Three attacks were
made on mission houses at the busy whaling
port of Lahaina on the island of Maui. The
Honolulu outrage did nothing to enhance the
repute of "Mad Jack" Percival.

It happened on a Sabbath. On Sunday,
February 26, 1826, a group of sailors from
the *Dolphin* broke into the house of Prime
Minister Kalanimoku, armed with clubs and
shouting, "Where are the women?" They
smashed the tall windows and yelled demands
for repeal of the edict against letting their
"wives" visit aboard.

From the first the men had received the
support of their captain, who had remonstated
with Kaahumanu and Boki about restricting
the old liberties. Percival accused the mission-

aries of meddling, but in sturdy Hiram Bingham he met a stubborn opponent. The chiefs and other Hawaiians stood on the sidelines, wondering why American sailors sent to protect their nation's interests in the Pacific should quarrel with American men of Christ.

More than a hundred men from the *Dolphin* and the whale ships in the harbor gathered at the fray. Boki told Bingham to go home to the stone cottage across the road, to protect his wife and child. On the way Hiram fell into the hands of the mob. One man whipped out a knife. When another aimed a blow at Bingham's head, Namahana, the portly sister of Kaahumanu, protected him until he could parry with his umbrella.

The watching Hawaiians then went into action, and many of the sailors would undoubtedly have been killed except that the missionaries and leading chiefs called out: "Tabu! Thou shalt not kill!"

Late on the scene, Captain Percival arrived with some of his midshipmen and began to lash about him with his whalebone cane. He spent an hour getting his unruly men back aboard. But he still called the edict against prostitution an insult to the Stars and Stripes. The upshot was that Percival had his way, and wahines by the score once more swam to the ships.

When John Percival returned to his home port in America he faced a court-martial for his behavior; but after due proceedings, he was acquitted because he had helped to quell the riot that his demands had caused. No wonder, though, that the *Dolphin* was always remembered by the Hawaiians as "the mischief-making man-of-war". Nowadays, however, a destroyer squadron based at Pearl Harbor annually celebrates a "Mad Jack Percival Day".

Relations with America were improved later in the same year, when Lieutenant Thomas ap Catesby Jones, who won the title of "the kind-eyed chief", arrived in the United States sloop of war *Peacock* and arranged a fair treaty between his country and the Hawaiian kingdom.

The *Dolphin* departed from Honolulu on May 11. On the return passage to South America, Percival first headed for the Society group. The crew sighted a low island early in June which they named Hull's Island; this was not the atoll in the Phoenix group named by Lieutenant Charles Wilkes in 1840, but perhaps Iles Maria, an outlier of the Tubuai or Austral group. A day later the

B

Dolphin sighted "Ramitaria" or Rimatara, and on the 13th made "Toubouai" or Tubuai. There Paulding had a chance to inspect the island where the mutineers of the *Bounty* had tried to settle but had fought with the inhabitants. Hiram became a "high carnie" or close friend of King Dick.

Seeking breadstuffs, the *Dolphin* touched on the 22nd at the dangerous high island of "Oparro" or Rapa. There, after difficulties with the coral reefs, the ship loaded some "mountain taro", a large root resembling a West Indian yam. After leaving Ilots de Bass (Morotiri), the Corones of Pedro Fernández de Quirós, the crew saw, during a run of 3,500 miles, no land until sighting Más a Fuera and Más a Tierra, better known as the Juan Fernández group. The latter island was the home for more than four years of Alexander Selkirk, the cranky Scottish carpenter who was the original of Defoe's Robinson Crusoe.

The *Dolphin* dropped anchor on July 23 in the harbor of Valparaiso, after eleven months on the loose in the South Seas. Paulding's concluding words stress the value of the crew's discoveries, especially for the whale ships that were to criss-cross the Pacific in later decades. Above all, he pointed out, American justice, although slow, was sure, for the crew, "in the hands of Providence and our government", had proved that crime could not go unpunished in the remotest part of the earth, and that no situation—such as that of Lay and Hussey—is so perilous as to justify despair.

The crew scattered. The celebrated castaways, Lay and Hussey, were turned over to Commodore Hull and returned in the *United States* to their homeland. They were never brought to trial on the charge of mutiny, and lived to publish their little book, *Narrative of the Mutiny on Board the Ship* "Globe"...(1828).

"Mad Jack" Percival, cleared by the court of inquiry on his actions at Honolulu, continued his naval career with distinction. He was made a commander in 1831 and a captain in 1841. He took the U.S.S. *Constitution* on a cruise around Africa to China and back by way of Hawaii and California from 1844 to 1846. He was put on the reserve list in 1855 and died when the Civil War was half over.

Hiram Paulding also continued in the sea service. He married in 1828 and reared six children between cruises. After his promotion to the rank of captain he made a China voyage in the U.S.S. *Vincennes* from 1844 to 1847. His sound judgment and even temper made him an excellent diplomat. As captain of the new frigate *St. Lawrence* he showed the flag in German and English ports. While in command of the Home Squadron he and his men bloodlessly captured General William Walker, the notorious American filibuster, and about 150 of his followers at Grey Town, Nicaragua. Hiram was active throughout the Civil War. John Ericsson, ship designer, wrote to him: "Without your firm support the *Monitor* would not have been built." Paulding's long and honorable career ended when he was a rear admiral, senior on the retired list and the last officer survivor of the Battle of Lake Champlain.

Paulding's prose is sailorly and straightforward, but he had a gift of selecting descriptive details that makes his *Dolphin* book good reading today. His amusing preface shows that he shared the wit of his kinsman, James Kirke Paulding, who collaborated with Washington Irving.

Many thanks are due to Miss Agnes Conrad and the Hawaiian Historical Society, which permitted its copy of Paulding's *Journal* to be photographed for the present edition.

A. GROVE DAY

University of Hawaii,
  Honolulu, 1970

SOME SOURCES

Bingham, Hiram, *A Residence of Twenty-one Years in the Sandwich Islands*. New York, 1847.

Davis, Charles Henry, *Life of Chas. Henry Davis, Rear-Admiral, 1807-1877*. New York, 1899, p. 32.

Johnson, Allan and Malone, Dumas, eds., *Dictionary of American Biography*, VII. New York, 1934. "Paulding" and "Percival."

Lay, William and Hussey, Cyrus, *A Narrative of the Mutiny on Board the Ship "Globe" of Nantucket . . .* New London, Conn., 1828.

Loomis, Albertine, *Grapes of Canaan*. New York, 1951, pp. 251–265.

Meade, Rebecca Paulding, *Life of Hiram Paulding, Rear-Admiral, U.S.N*. New York, 1910.

Michener, James A. and Day, A. Grove, *Rascals in Paradise*. New York, 1957, Chapter I.

JOURNAL

OF A

CRUISE

OF THE

UNITED STATES SCHOONER DOLPHIN,

AMONG THE ISLANDS OF THE PACIFIC OCEAN;

AND A VISIT TO THE MULGRAVE ISLANDS,

IN PURSUIT OF THE MUTINEERS OF THE

WHALE SHIP GLOBE.

WITH A MAP.

By Lieut. HIRAM PAULDING, of the U. S. Navy.

NEW-YORK:

G. & C. & H. CARVILL.

M,DCCC,XXXI.

NEW-YORK:

LUDWIG & TOLEFREE, PRINTERS,
No. 72, Vesey-street.

PREFACE.

———

THE principal inducement of the author, in preparing the following Journal for publication, originated in an idea that a plain narrative of a a cruise through an unfrequented part of the ocean, comprising a particular description of a groupe of Islands, never before explored, and forming, perhaps, the latest inhabited portion of the globe, might not be without interest. It is believed, that, in habits, opinions, and modes of living, the people of the Mulgrave Islands, approach more nearly to a state of nature than those of any other known region. The object of the CRUISE, of which a concise account is now offered to the Public, necessarily led to a more full examination of these Islands than has yet been made, or than it will ever probably be thought worth while to make again, except for a similar purpose.

The delay in publishing this little work originated partly in the hesitation of the author in offering, and partly in that of the booksellers, in accepting it; and the public must decide whether they were not both right in the first instance. It only remains for him to state, that all he aimed at or desired, was to give a plain, unpretending narrative, of what he saw, which, without presuming to merit applause, might at least escape censure.

New-York, May, 1831.

JOURNAL

OF A

CRUISE OF THE U.S. SCHOONER DOLPHIN.

In the year 1824, the crew of a whale ship, called the Globe, belonging to the island of Nantucket, mutinied while in the Pacific Ocean, murdered the officers in latitude about eight degrees south, longitude one hundred and sixty degrees west, and carried the ship to the Mulgrave Islands, where it was proposed by the chief mutineers to burn her, and form a settlement. Here they landed a great part of the stores, sails, rigging, &c.; but some of the crew, who had no part in the mutiny, taking advantage of the others' being on shore, cut the cables, just at the dusk of evening, and, making sail, stood out to sea with a fine breeze.

The mutineers pursued the ship, as soon as they discovered she was underway, but, finding that she outsailed them, they soon gave up the chase, and returned to the shore. The nautical instruments of every description had been taken on shore by order of the mutineers, so that the people on board of the Globe were left to traverse a vast ocean, studded with islands, and rocks, and reefs, where currents are frequent, strong, and variable, without any other guide by which to direct their course than the stars and prevailing winds. The Mulgrave Islands are situated in north latitude six degrees, east longitude one hundred and seventy-three degrees; and although the passage of the Globe was very long, she arrived safely at Valparaiso, where the crew informed the American Consul of the events that had transpired. It was unfortunately at a period when our commerce, on the coast of the Pacific, required for its protection all the naval force we had at the time on that station, and no measures were taken to bring the offenders to answer for their crimes, until some months after the Globe had returned to the United States. Information of the occurrence having been communicated to the secretary of the navy, he, in 1825, directed Commodore Hull, then commanding our squadron in the Pacific Ocean, to despatch the United States schooner Dolphin, in search of such of the mutineers as had been left at the Mulgraves. Besides the importance of bringing the guilty to punishment, for the sake of example,—humanity for the suffering condition of the innocent, that had been left by those who escaped, dictated that something should be done for their relief. Accordingly on the 18th of August, 1825, the Dolphin sailed from Chorillos, on the coast of Peru, under the command of Lieutenant Percival, who was directed, preparatory to his departure from the coast, to stop at some convenient place for such refreshments as might be necessary for the cruise. On the day following, we stood into the harbour of Casma, and anchored, when we fired several guns, as signals, to acquaint the people in the interior of the arrival of a stranger that wanted their aid. It was not long before we had the satisfaction of seeing a number of people, who had made their appearance in obedience to the signal. A few moments' conversation with them, satisfied us that our wants could not be supplied here. Wood might have been obtained, but the water was neither good, nor convenient to be got at, and all other things that we were in want of, could only be procured at the most extravagant prices.

After laying at anchor a few hours, we got underway, and stood along the coast for a small place called Santa, which was situated a few leagues to the north of us. Casma is but a poor harbour, as it lies so much exposed to the prevailing southerly winds, that frequently a high and dangerous surf breaks upon that part of the shore where alone (at any time) it is practicable to land.

A valley, covered with thickets of reeds and bushes, extends back from the sea for several miles. In it there is neither habitations nor inhabitants, and a sandy waste of hill and dale separates it from the little Indian village of Casma, which is several miles in the interior. It is situated in a valley, about a league in circumference, which is watered by a small stream. The soil is rich, but poorly cultivated. The inhabitants (of whom there is about a thousand) are all Indians. They live in wretched habitations, and their intercourse with the Spaniards for centuries, it seems, has not much improved their condition in any respect. Their principal dependance is upon the sale of their poultry to such ships as visit their harbour for the trade of the interior country, and to people thus engaged, their proximity may sometimes be a very great convenience.

The harbour of Santa is formed by several small islands, lying a little to the south of it, and about a mile from the main. We passed between the islands and the main, although it was night, and very dark. On the following morning, we made the customary signal, by firing a gun, which, in a very short time, brought the captain of the port down to the beach. He had not much the appearance of official dignity, having a long black beard, and was in no respect prepossessing. Rude, however, as was his exterior, he was profuse in offers of hospitality. He assured us that we should be abundantly supplied with every thing we wanted, and requested that an officer might be sent with him to Santa, to negociate for our supplies. The purser and myself were ordered upon this service, and not having time to send to Santa for horses, it being six miles from our anchorage, we were reduced to the necessity of a most painful ride, behind the captain of the port and a companion whom he had brought with him. The road was over an uninterrupted plain, which was almost everywhere covered with impenetrable thickets of reeds, and the Algaroba*, and in some places a foot or two deep with water that had escaped from the streams of the cultivated valley. When we arrived at the door of the commandant's house, he shewed us in with an air of some formality, and welcomed us with every Spanish expression of hospitality. The appearance of the house corresponded well with that of its occupant. It was disgusting in the extreme. There were but two rooms in it, one of which was occupied as a granary and bed-room, and the other as a pulparia,† and the ordinary conveniences of the family. In the middle of the latter, hung a hog, weighing three or four hundred pounds, which had been butchered that morning. The captain pretended

* A tree that resembles the locust. It bears a pod, like that of a bean, which is given by the Peruvians to their horses.

† A retail grocery and tippling shop.

he could himself supply whatever we asked for, assuring us that he would sell more cheaply than any one else, and evinced an extreme jealousy at our conversing with any other than himself upon the subject of our visit to Santa. As a matter of courtesy, we soon made our way to the house of the governor, and paid our respects to him. He seemed to feel highly complimented with our attention, and, like the captain of the port, proffered his assistance to obtain for us whatever we stood in need of. He bore the name of the cruel conqueror of Peru, it being nothing less than the great Pizarro; but it was evident, from his complexion and curling locks, that his ancestors came from Africa. Notwithstanding this disadvantage, however, he could not be compared to the captain of the port without disparagement, and, considering the wretched society in which he lived, I thought he discharged his official duties rather creditably. Both the governor and captain of the port invited us to dine with them; and each, fearing we would make our purchase of the other, solicited our company very earnestly. We finally accepted the invitation of the latter, and he escorted us back to his house, where the table was already smoking with savoury dishes, served up in a variety of ways from the huge animal we had seen there in the morning, under circumstances by no means calculated to improve our appetites. A rabble, formed of half naked Indians, and long bearded white men, assembled in the room, while we were at dinner, some of whom sat down at table unceremoniously, and partook with us. Our host indulged himself freely with the use of aqua-diente,* and, ere we finished our repast, his house exhibited a constant scene of riot, from which we were exceedingly glad to escape. After making a few purchases we returned on board. The next day, a party, consisting of about thirty or forty, came down to make us a visit. All degrees of the society of Santa, without any distinction,— whites, mulattoes, and Indians, having, it would seem, mingled together for the occasion. They remained with us all day, eating and drinking, and appeared to be very happy; but begged for every thing that came in their way. At sunset, to our great satisfaction, they left us, and on the following morning, we got underway, and continued along the coast to the north.

The small town of Santa contains about two thousand inhabitants, nearly all of whom are Indians. It is situated in latitude nine degrees south, in the valley of Santa, which is twenty or thirty miles in circumference, beautiful and rich in soil, and watered by a deep and rapid stream, which takes its rise in the Andes, at the distance of a hundred miles from the sea coast. Previous to

C * Spirits distilled from the grape.

the revolution, it was a flourishing valley, with a numerous population, producing rice, wheat, and other grain, in considerable quantities, for exportation; and frequently large herds of cattle were driven from it to Lima. It abounds also in fruits, such as oranges, lemons, grapes, and a variety of other delicious kinds. Large farming establishments are every where to be seen, each comprehending thousands of acres, and previous to the revolution possessed by gentlemen of ample fortune. All of these are now in ruins, and most of them unoccupied. The climate of Santa is mild, and almost unvarying. Here, as in nearly all the rest of Peru, bordering on the Pacific Ocean, it never rains, and wherever the land is cultivated it is watered from the rivers.

Around the cultivated valley of Santa, are spread extensive plains of barren sand; and at a short distance back from the sea rises the first range of gloomy and sterile mountains which, increasing in altitude as you advance into the interior, terminates in the eternal snow-covered Andes, at the distance of from fifty to a hundred miles. At Santa we obtained wood with ease, and from two or three old wells, near the shore, filled our casks with brackish water. Where the river empties into the harbour it is so much exposed to the sea as to render watering difficult, and almost always dangerous. Santa was a place of some trade before the revolution, it being connected by direct communication with some mines of the precious metals in the interior.

On the 24th of August, we anchored in the roads of Huanchaco, and com municated with several vessels that were lying there. Huanchaco is an Indian village, and the seaport of the city of Bolivia, the ancient name of which was Truxillo. It is exposed to the sea, and at times the surf breaks so violently on the shore, as to prevent all intercourse with the vessels at anchor. The Indians are provided with a float they call Balsa, and on which they pass through this surf, in cases of great emergency, when no boat could live in it. It is composed merely of two bundles of long reeds, bound compactly together, tapering a little at one end, and the two bundles secured to each other, the small ends coming to a point, somewhat resembling in appearance the bow of a boat. In the middle it is hollowed sufficiently for a man to seat himself securely. It is usually about fifteen feet long, and from two to three feet wide. It is calculated for one man only, who directs it with his paddle. I one day witnessed their wonderful skill in the management of the balsa. The surf was breaking so furiously, that the men, accustomed to work in it, advised me not to go on board of my ship. Whilst I was standing on the shore, with several

of them around me, a boat appeared just without
the heavy rollers that were setting in, filled with
people, who it was evident were strangers to the
danger they were about to encounter, as they were
dashing on fearlessly into the surf.   The Indians
near me made motions, and called to them not to
advance further, but they neither saw nor heard
the warning.   Observing this, six or eight of
them launched their balsas, and in a few minutes
were in the midst of the breakers.   They were
just in time, for the boat in a moment afterwards
darted forward with great velocity, and suddenly
disappeared.   The wave had broken, and was
foaming over her, and another must have terminated the existence of every person on board;
but, before the next swell, that came rolling on in
quick succession had reached them, each man was
upon a balsa, and the skilful and intrepid Indians
bore them safely to the shore.   We remained but
a few hours at Huanchaco, when we continued on
to the north, and on the 25th of August, came up
with the Lobos Islands, in latitude six degrees
south, and distant about a hundred miles from the
coast.   They are barren rocks, rising in some
places several hundred feet, and no where have any
appearance of vegetation.   With the aid of our
glasses, we saw at a distance a number of people
upon these inhospitable rocks, and supposing they
might be some unfortunate seamen, whose vessel

had been cast away, we hove to, with a view of affording them relief. Upon examination, however, they proved to be Indians from the coast, who had come here on a catamaran, upon a fishing enterprise, it being the season when great quantities of fish, resembling mackerel, are taken on the shores of these Islands.

Previous to ascertaining who these fishermen were, we landed on a small island nearer to us, where, on the side of a hill, forty or fifty yards distant, we saw several hundreds of seals basking in the sun. The rock rose perhaps a hundred feet, and many of the seals were near the top of it. The noise of our landing gave them the alarm, and, as we had cut them off from the water, they made the best of their way for the other side of the hill, joining in a terrific growl like so many furious mastiffs. They had reached the top of the hill, and were descending on the opposite side, when we overtook them, and very wantonly killed several. They were so large that many of them would have weighed at least five or six hundred pounds, but their motions were extremely clumsy. Whenever we came near them they would growl, and snapped at us like a ferocious dog, and their long teeth warned us not to approach them within striking distance. Considering their immense size, it is astonishing how slight a blow will kill them when given on the nose. If, however, this fatal part is missed, and they receive a severe blow upon any other part of the head, they suffer but little injury, and become extremely tenacious of life, particularly if it has time to swell. The nose is then no longer a mortal part, and it is almost impossible to subdue them. We witnessed several instances of this kind, being but poorly provided with weapons proper for the purpose, and withal unskilled in the use of them. In descending from the top of the hill, there was but one narrow defile by which they could escape, and there they floundered for nearly half an hour, tumbling over each other three or four deep, until at last they got into their native element.

The north side of the Lobos Islands affords a fine harbour, where we saw a small vessel at anchor waiting for the proceeds of her cargo, which had been landed on the coast at a place called Lambayaca.

On the 26th of August, we anchored at Peyta, in latitude five degrees south. This was the last place at which it would be convenient for us to stop, and here, to our gratification, we were enabled to obtain the necessary refreshments for our cruise. We filled the deck with pigs, poultry, and vegetables, and at considerable expense succeeded, after much trouble, in obtaining a supply of good water. Peyta is situated in a deep bay, and is a good harbour, formed by two projecting points of land, and is for many leagues surrounded by barren sand. It is the seaport of an interior city, called Pieura, and receives from distant valleys all that is necessary for the consumption of the inhabitants or strangers, who visit it for the purposes of trade. It is supplied with water from a river that empties itself into the sea, near a small Indian town called Colan, whence we found it necessary to resort for a supply. When we had proceeded there, and anchored our vessel within a mile or two of the town, the only method by which we could obtain water, was to have it brought in calabashes on mules. It was their saint's day, and in the village all was frolic and mirth. Groups of men and women were every where seen, dressed fantastically, singing and dancing along the streets. I called upon the governor, who was a white man, very early in the morning, to report the arrival of our vessel, and the object of our visit. He had just risen from his hammock, and received me with many expressions of civility, and proffers of assistance. His house was but little better than that of the captain of the port of Santa, and his appearance not more prepossessing. The room into which I was ushered had no other floor than the ground beaten hard, on which were several large piles of pumpkins, bags of beans, and Indian corn, which he proposed to sell me before our official interview had ended.

Immediately after breakfast he came on board to visit the captain, bringing with him several emales. They remained on board nearly all day, to the annoyance of every body, and in the evening were removed to the shore with great difficulty, so freely had they partaken of our hospitality. Soon after our arrival at Peyta, we were invited to dine with the governor, who treated us with great kindness and hospitality. Some months previous to our arrival, his son had shipped himself at Talcahuana, on board of the Dolphin, as a common sailor, and was discharged on our arrival here, and permitted to remain with his friends. He was spoken of amongst us as a person who had been compelled to fly from his home for improper conduct of some kind, and now the whole mystery was explained. His father was one of the most respectable and patriotic men in the place where he resided; but this son was a youth of a bad disposition, and had given him a great deal of trouble. When the revolution first commenced in that section of the country, he provided himself with the uniform of a patriot officer, and went about the country, where he was a stranger, or but slightly known, and under the authority of his pretended commission, took, by violence, the cattle and horses of the farmers, or whatever else he could possess himself of, which he converted into money for his own purposes. Sometimes he even pressed the Indians as soldiers, and compelled them to assist him in carrying off his plunder.

At length, his exactions became so heavy, and were levied so tyrannically, that a gentleman resisted him, and questioned the legality of his authority. Numbers were fired with indignation against him, and the propriety of his conduct was no sooner questioned, than the investigation was followed up with such activity, that, finding there was no safety but in flight, he preferred a voluntary exile to meeting the just resentment of the people he had injured. He had suffered many hardships during his absence, and appeared on his return to be truly penitent. I was at his father's house when he entered. His mother and sisters were deeply affected, and received him with all the tenderness of female sympathy, their eyes overflowing with tears. They each embraced him, as one most dear to them; but when he approached his father (a man about sixty) who was standing on the opposite side of the room, he caught the old man's eye bent indignantly upon him, and turned away with a look humbled to the dust.

Whilst lying here we had an opportunity of witnessing a solitary instance of an enterprising disposition in a Peruvian Indian,—a characteristic, it is believed, they but rarely possess, or, at most, but in a slight degree. We had on board an Indian youth, who belonged to this part of Peru, and for several days had held frequent conversations with his countrymen, who were attracted on board by curiosity. One of these people had concerted with the youth a plan for his deserting. In compliance with this arrangement, he put off, during the mid-watch, with his canoe, and taking his station just ahead of the Dolphin, gave a shrill whistle as the signal of his approach. The lad, fearing that he might be detected, did not venture to answer the signal, which was repeated several times, when the officer of the watch suspecting the object, gave the long expected response, and the credulous Indian came cautiously paddling close under the bow of the vessel, where, to his amazement, he was made prisoner, and compelled to go on board. When the captain came on deck the next morning, he punished the poor Indian, by impressing upon him the belief that he intended to detain, and make a soldier of him. Not having sagacity enough to know the difference between our vessel and a patriot man-of-war, and conceiving that there was no chance for his escape, he made the most pathetic appeals to the captain's humanity, and appeared to suffer all the agony of despair. The captain ordered a cartridge-box to be put over his shoulders, and a musket placed in his hands.

He seemed frantic with the reality of his servitude, using his utmost violence to disengage himself from the cartridge-box and musket, declaring again and again that he was no soldier, and in the most affecting manner begging the captain for God's sake to permit him to go on shore. When his tormentors discontinued their persecutions, he jumped over the stern into his canoe, with great activity, and soon joined his anxious friends on the beach, who had assembled there, apprehensive of his captivity, and awaiting the result.

On the 2d of September, we sailed from Peyta, and shaped our course for the Gallapagos Islands. The trade wind was moderate, accompanied with fine weather. On the morning of the 6th, we made Hood's Island, and in a few hours afterwards, anchored on the west side, in a small harbour, called Gardner's Bay, the only one it affords. After dinner, the captain took with him twenty or thirty of the crew, and went in pursuit of turtle. The island is high and mountainous, covered every where with volcanic cinders, many of which are in huge masses. The men were at first very eager in their search for turtle, and the whole crew, if they had been permitted, would gladly have engaged in it.

They expected to have found the turtle near the shore; instead of which they had to scramble over rocks and climb mountains, half the time making their way through brambles, at the expense of scratches and torn clothes. Men were never more disappointed than our crew in the amusement of catching turtle. Sometimes they would wander about for hours before they found one, and then it would probably be a mile or two from the beach, and as much as a man could well lift. By sundown we had collected about thirty, of large size. Black grouper were very abundant close to our anchorage, but the sharks were so numerous that for every fish taken we lost one or two hooks. We got a plentiful supply for the crew, however, in the course of an hour. On the following morning, we joined Captain Meek, of the brig Tamahamah, which vessel had accompanied us hither, and making a large party—went round the island about ten or twelve miles from our anchorage, where we expected to find turtle more abundant. The captain was an old cruiser here, and well calculated to make one of an agreeable party. He stood cook for us, and as the day was very warm, our first essay on landing, was to make a large bower, under which to prepare our dinner. The people then dispersed, to look for turtle, the first of which were served up for our dinner, in a style that might have been relished by less keen appetites than ours, which were sharpened by laborious exercise. At night, we had collected upwards of a hundred, besides ten large green turtle, we were so fortunate as to find on the beach near the place of our landing. When we came to assemble our men to return on board, two of them were missing, and upon inquiry were ascertained to have been absent nearly all day. We dispersed and looked for them in every direction until dark, when every body being much fatigued, a party was left to search for them again in the morning, and the rest repaired on board. In the morning, we renewed our labours without success, and with great reason began to feel seriously alarmed for the safety of our shipmates. There was no water on the island, and the preceding day had been so extremely warm, that we feared the poor fellows would soon perish, if they had not already. Our search, too, was attended with considerable danger. Wandering about in distant parts of the island, we sometimes, in clambering over rocks and mountains, changed our course without being sensible of it, and would find ourselves pursuing our way in a different direction from what we supposed. In the afternoon, when our strength and patience were quite exhausted, and our parties returning for the night, the lost men suddenly appeared on the beach, close to the vessel. They were pale and emaciated, with scarcely strength to move one foot before the other. Their clothes were in tatters, and their shoes worn off their feet, which were very much crippled with their long journey over the sharp cinders. It appeared from the story of these men,

that they had several times been on· the side of
the island where we were anchored, but upon an
eminence that overlooked the vessel, and thinking
themselves on the other side, recrossed; when, to
their astonishment, seeing nothing of her, they
would retrace their steps; and in this manner,
were wandering about for many hours, almost
despairing at last of finding relief. While they
were in this wretched situation, they several times
quenched their thirst by killing turtle that came in
their way, and drinking from the reservoir with
which nature has supplied this singular animal.
I have since been told by a seaman, that he deserted from a whale ship at these islands, accompanied
by a number of others, and that for weeks, they
had no other water than what they obtained by
breaking open the turtles and drinking of the
water they found in them. It is contained in a
pouch that resembles a bladder, and is immediately connected with the stomach. It is large in
proportion to the size of the animal, and some of
them will hold two or three gallons. It surprised
us to see the tameness of the birds. They would
scarcely fly from us when we approached them
within a few feet, and in many instances we could
pick them up with our hands. The gannet, generally of a clear white, and as large as a goose, we
could catch with great ease; and the albatrosses,
some grey and some yellow, which were much

larger than any bird we have in the United States, would but rarely rise upon the wing to escape us. They ran very fast, and would sometimes give us a chase of one or two hundred yards. A bird, the plumage and form of which differed in no respect from our mocking-bird, would feed within a few feet of us, and the turtle-doves were killed in great numbers by our people, with short poles. Hood's Island is evidently of volcanic origin. It is, indeed, nothing but a mass of cinders. It is covered with a slight growth of scrubby bushes of various kinds, and occasionally a tree of four or five inches in diameter, is met with. Of all its vegetation, the cactus seems best adapted to it. There is a variety of the species; one of which attains to a larger size than any other production of the island, and spreads out into a tree of considerable height. This kind of the cactus is chosen by the turtle for food. When the whalers, or other visiters, go to the Gallapagos Islands for these animals, they cut down a number of the trees in the evening, and on the following morning they are sure to find turtle feeding there, although none could be seen in its vicinity on the preceding day. The guanas are not the least remarkable of the inhabitants of the Gallapagos. They are from two to three feet long and shaped like a lizard. Their colour varies from grey to jet black. They are

easily caught and quite harmless; are often
eaten and said to be excellent. On the top of the
head they have a beautiful shining crest of black
and yellow, which, in the sun, has a most brilliant
appearance.

Except where we anchored, a heavy surf breaks
all round Hood's Island, In a high and central
part of it, is a place which resembles the dry bed
of a small lake. It is surrounded by ridges and
peaks of cinders rising in some places from one to
three hundred feet, and in all probability has been
the crater of a volcano. In places difficult of
access we saw a few seals, but so shy that with
the exception of one or two instances, we could
not approach them. The few that we killed were
hair seal, and consequently of but little value.
Between Hood's Island and the small one that
forms the harbour, there is a passage for ships,
but it is very narrow, and with a strong current
that runs through it, which would always render
it dangerous for a ship to attempt to pass, particularly so if the wind were not perfectly fair.

At one, P. M., on the 10th of September, we got
underway, and stood over for Charles Island,
where we anchored at six, in Essex Bay. Rock
Dismal, so called by Commodore Porter, is an excellent land mark, and seems to have been appro-
priately named. It rises to the eastward of Essex

Bay, in sharp crags of fifty to a hundred feet high.
A few solitary bushes constitute all its vegetation.
In approaching Essex Bay, and at its entrance,
we were alarmed several times by a strong ripple,
but in casting the lead found no bottom with ten
fathoms of line. At Essex Bay, is the celebrated
post-office of the whalers, to which Commodore
Porter resorted several times during his cruise
for information. We found a letter there left by
a whaler who had visited Charles Island for a supply of turtle. He was last from the river Tumbez,
where one of his crew had caught a fever, of
which he died. Two others lost their way in the
mountains of Charles Island, where, after wandering about for a considerable time, one of them
complained to his companion of a head-ache, and
soon after sat down and died. The other found
his way to the ship after a great deal of suffering.

Charles Island is high and mountainous, and like
Hood's, is covered with a thin growth of bushes.
At the distance of a mile from the beach there is a
small spring of water, to which there is a footpath
over the crags and hills, worn by visiters in search
of turtle, a scanty supply of which can only be
obtained with great labour. The residence of
Pat, the Irishman, in this lone and dreary place,
for a number of years, has made it an object of
curiosity to all who visit the island. Here he
planted his potatoes and pumpkins, and raised

D

his chickens; administering the government of his island with despotic sway, for Pat was a monarch although he pillowed his head upon a rock, and reposed his rude limbs on a bed made of bushes. The story is known to all who have read Commodore Porter's journal, in which he gives an account of Pat's residence on this island, and of his possessing himself of the person and services of a black man belonging to a whale ship, who had strayed too far from his companions, and whom Pat held in durance for a long time.

At ten, A. M., we parted company with the Tamahamah, and sailed for the Marqueses Islands. The turtle with which our deck was covered, were very troublesome and offensive for about a week, when they became quite domesticated and gave us not the slightest inconvenience. For two or three weeks we served them to the crew constantly, in lieu of the usual allowance of salt provisions. It was a most valuable substitute, and important to us, as we were bound upon a long cruise, as well for the health of the crew as for the preservation of our sea stock. When the number became comparatively small, we discontinued the general use of them, and served them only once or twice a week. We never fed them, and for aught I could see, they were equally as fat and healthy a month after they were taken on board, as on the first day. As a sea stock nothing can be more convenient or better calculated for a long cruise. They may be put any where and kept in almost any way, and if it should be thought advisable to feed them, there is scarcely any vegetable substance that they will not eat after they are a little domesticated. The liver of this turtle is particularly delicious. When fried, it is not unlike a fine oyster, and although partaken very freely of, no ill effect is ever experienced from it. Sixteen days after leaving Charles Island, we made the island Rooahooga, one of the southernmost of the Marqueses group. The wind was fresh and blew steadily from the southward and eastward, accompanied by a heavy swell. As we approached the islands, we had some rainy and cloudy weather, but with this exception, our whole passage was attended with clear days and fine moonlight nights. In latitude three degrees south, and longitude ninety-five degrees west, we observed a remarkable appearance in the water, which, had we been navigating an unfrequented ocean, would have very much alarmed us. At several different times during the day, on September 12th, we passed through violent rips, and at times nearly the whole ocean assumed the appearance and agitation of boiling water.

Throughout our passage, we remarked, that whenever the wind hauled to the southward of

southeast, it increased in force.   It occurred so
frequently as to be a subject of general remark.

On the 20th of September, in latitude seven degrees fifty minutes south, and longitude one hundred and twenty degrees thirty minutes west, we
saw a comet for the first time, thirty or forty degrees above the horizon, and bearing from us east
by north.   At day-light, on the morning of September 26th, several of the southernmost of the
Marqueses were in sight.   They were all mountainous, but covered with vegetation, and as we
drew near presented a pleasing contrast to the
sterile and gloomy Gallapagos.   We stood along
the shore of La Dominica, admiring the beautiful
little valleys that were presented to our view in
quick succession, where villages of palm-thatched
huts, surrounded by clumps of tall cocoa-nut and
wide-spreading bread fruit trees, formed scenes of
rural quiet calculated to fill the imagination with
the most agreeable conceptions of the happy condition of their inhabitants.   At length we came to
a small bay where the valley was more populous
than any we had seen before, and the captain, to
our great satisfaction, hauled up for it and stood
close in towards the island.   We lowered a boat,
and providing ourselves with a few trifles for presents, pulled into the bay within a few yards of
the shore.   The beach was already thronged with
people of all ages, male and female, who invited

us to land by the most significant gestures, whilst
many of them were singing and dancing to express
their joy. The surrounding rocks and hills were
covered with groups of females, gaily decked off
with their neat head-dresses of the white Tapa
cloth and many-coloured robes, which were float-
ing in the wind, half concealing and half exposing
their fantastically painted limbs. When they saw
that we would not land, the men and boys dashed
into the water with whatever they had to offer us,
and swam off to the boat. A chief, who had a dry
wreath of cocoa-nut around his brows, came off
with them; and, upon being invited, got into the
boat, where he remained until our departure, apparently giving orders from time to time to those
who were passing and repassing from the shore to
the boat. In a few minutes, they had presented us
with a considerable quantity of cocoa-nuts, bananas, and papayas, for which we gave them in return
a few trifling articles, the most valuable of which
were glass beads. The chief had his eyes constantly fixed upon our fire-arms, and finally gave
us to understand, by motions, that a pistol would
be acceptable to him. With this intimation we
could not comply; but he bore the refusal with
great good nature, and for some time after our
store of little presents was exhausted, his people
continued to bring us off fruit without the expectation of any return. When they found that we

were serious in our refusal to land, the women came from the hills and assembled on the rocks close to us, where, in a nearer view, they could display their persons to more advantage, and charm us with the melody of their voices. There they all joined in songs, keeping time by clapping their hands, stopping occasionally to receive the applause of the men and to invite us on shore. Several of them, male and female, swam off to the boat; and when we were about to depart, insisted so strongly upon going on board with us that we had to use some violence to get clear of them.

We continued on in the afternoon, soon passing La Dominica, and at sundown made Rooahooga ahead. The weather being squally and the island only fifteen miles from us, we lay by for the night. At daylight, we found ourselves a few miles distant from the middle of the south side of the island, where a bay presented itself, which, at a distance, promised to afford anchorage. On a nearer approach, however, its appearance changed, and as there were but few signs of inhabitants, we ran along toward the west end of the island. This part of it had not much appearance of fertility, although we saw a few large trees. It is high, broken, and indented with a number of small bays, none of which are large enough to form a harbour. In rounding the southwest point of the island we had sudden and violent gusts of wind. Invisible

Bay is situated a little to the westward of this point, and although it has somewhat the appearance of a harbour, and presents to view a beautiful sand beach, we saw no indications of inhabitants. About ten miles to the north, we anchored in twenty fathoms water, having rocky bottom, and an inaccessible rocky shore where the surf breaks violently. The captain and several officers went back to Invisible Bay in one of the boats, and in a cave close to the shore they found five or six natives, who at their approach, fled to the hills, making signs for our people to depart. In the cave, they found a few fishing-nets. They tried to prevail upon the natives to come near, but their demonstrations of friendship were answered only by motions expressive of hostility. The landing was difficult, as the shore was rocky, and a considerable surf broke upon it, although the bay was tolerably protected by a projecting point. Soon after meridian, we got under way and shaped our course for Nooaheeva, which was plainly in sight from Rooahooga. We stood along, with a fine breeze and clear weather, and at three, P. M., rounded the northeastern extremity of Nooaheeva, when a spacious harbour, called Comptroller's Bay, opened to our view. It is about three miles deep, and at its inner extremity are two projecting points that extend out for more than a mile, and form three

small harbours. We were no sooner observed by
the natives on shore, than they put off in a number
of large canoes and pulled with great rapidity
towards us. The wind was light and baffling,
and we advanced slowly into the harbour. In
a few minutes, we were surrounded by canoes,
containing from six to eight men each. They belonged to different tribes, which they attempted to
explain to us with great earnestness of speech and
gesture, but as we had no one on board who knew
much of the language, we were greatly at a loss
to comprehend their meaning. They had not followed us long when two of the canoes came along
side, one on each quarter, and the men crawled up
the side and perched themselves upon the ham-
mocks, like so many monkeys, where they called
out in a loud voice, addressing themselves alternately to us and to the natives on the side of the
vessel opposite to them,—one party exclaiming
"Mattee, mattee, Typee!" and the other "Mattee,
mattee,* Happah!" and occasionally using angry
gestures with the exclamation. This was too expressive for us not to understand. They belonged
to different tribes, the Typee, and Happah; and
were mutually trying to prejudice us against the
tribe to which they did not belong, in order to induce us to anchor in their own bay. Both the
bays were beautiful, but as the Happahs' was the

* Mattee, mattee—Very bad.

most populous and nearest to us, we gave it the preference; and a little before sunset anchored in twenty fathoms water within a cable's length of the shore. The Typees no sooner saw that we were standing in for the Happah Bay, than they hurried into their canoe and paddled off for their village as fast as they could. The Happah valley was a romantic spot. A plain, a league or two in circumference, stretched back to the mountains in a semicircular form, presenting in front a clear white sand beach about a mile long. The plain was covered with cocoa-nuts, with bread-fruit interspersed, and near enough to form a continued shade without presenting the appearance of a dense forest. Scattered about every where through these trees were the palm-thatched habitations of the natives. In the rear of the plain, the mountains rose precipitously, forming an insuperable barrier against the incursions of other tribes. The land rose gently to the left, but it was almost barren and added nothing to the beauty of the landscape. On the extreme right, a considerable mountain and a point projecting far out into the bay, separated the Happahs from the tribes that lived beyond them in that direction. Nothing could equal the apparent joy of the natives when they saw us anchored in front of their village. The whole tribe, which probably did not exceed five hundred, flocked down to the beach, expressing their satisfaction by dancing and singing. Hundreds of them dashed into the water and swam off to us, so that we had not time to furl sails and clear the deck before the vessel was crowded with people. To show them that we had the means of making successful resistance against any hostile intention they might adopt, we paraded our musketeers upon the deck and practised them, a ceremony that appeared to afford the natives very great amusement. We allowed them to remain on board until the dusk of evening, when the number being so great as to make the vessel uncomfortable, and apprehending that in the course of the night they might appropriate to themselves many things that they would find about the deck, and which could not conveniently be spared, we sent most of them on shore. The chiefs and a few others who expressed a great desire to remain, were permitted to pass the night with us.

On the following day, I took a few presents with me and went over to the Typee valley, to visit that tribe, celebrated as the most warlike of Nooaheeva. As soon as the boat was perceived, the people came running towards the beach in every direction, and before she reached the shore we were surrounded by great numbers, who plunged into the water and swam off to us. As many as we could conveniently accommodate were permitted to get into the boat, where they treated me so unceremoniously that I did not think it prudent to land. Amongst those who paid me a visit was a chief of the tribe. He was a man about thirty years of age, well-featured and of fine proportions. His deportment was grave and dignified, but like the rest of our new acquaintances, who swam off to us, he was quite naked except a slight covering about his loins. The common people treated him with great deference, and never intruded upon that part of the boat where he was seated. He made us understand that he wished to obtain muskets and powder, for the purchase of which he had caused five or six large hogs to be brought down, that were tied and laying on the shore. I offered him whatever else I had that I thought would induce him to part with them; but he obstinately refused any other consideration than muskets and powder. Large quantities of cocoanuts, bananas, and papayas were thrown into the boat by the people who were swimming around us, and when we had been lying there an hour, we had as many in the boat as we could conveniently carry. I had a variety of presents, such as beads, buttons, &c., all of which the common people were very anxious to obtain; but the chief would take nothing from me of less consequence than fire-arms or gunpowder. I offered him flints and musket balls, which, although of great value amongst the natives, he would not receive. He invited me frequently, with great earnestness of manner, to land, until he found, by my repeated refusals, that I was determined to remain in my boat.

The bay of the Typees was rather smaller than that of the Happah tribe. They live principally upon the side of a mountain that rises gently from the shore. The number of the tribe appeared to be about the same as that of the Happahs. Their houses are situated in circular chains of villages, rising one above the other, from the base to near the top of the mountain, where it terminates in rude and uninhabitable cliffs. Groves and clumps of cocoa-nut, and bread-fruit trees are every where interspersed with the dwellings, and the mind of the observer being impressed with the idea of their usefulness to the natives, gives a double effect to the beautiful landscape adorned by their waving tops and broad green leaves. We had several occasions to remark the inveterate dislike that the Typees and Happahs entertained towards each other.

On the morning after our arrival, the sailing-master went on shore in the Happah valley to obtain an altitude of the sun by the artificial horizon He was shy of the natives, as we all were at first, and apprehending that some of them might approach him with a hostile intention, while his back was turned towards them, and having heard that they held in great reverence a place said to be Tabooed, or consecrated, he made a circle round his place observation, and told the natives, who had followed him in great numbers, that the space within the circle was Tabooed. They stared at him in silence and stood back from it; but by and by, when he was intently engaged in getting his altitude, one of the natives, supposing that he was employed in some plan (to him incomprehensible) to destroy the Typees, as he turned the face of his sextant in that direction, crawled up gently behind the sailing-master, without being perceived by him, and suddenly tapping him two or three times on the shoulder, exclaimed with great energy, " Mattee, mattee, Typee !" It may readily be supposed that his imagination, which was very much excited before, was not soothed by this salutation. He turned upon the native, expressing in look and manner his consternation and displeasure, which was only met by the delighted Indian with a repetition of " Mattee, mattee, Typee !"

On the morning of the 25th, I went on shore, in company with several of the officers, to indulge our curiosity and ramble about the valley. We were soon surrounded by a group of natives, who followed us wherever we went. Our first object was to visit the chief of the valley, whose residence we found at the distance of two or three huudred

yards from the shore.   It was a plain, oblong hut,
thirty by twenty feet.   Its simple structure was
such as is first suggested to the untutored mind—
a few poles laid over crotches, upon which was
framed a triangular roof, and the whole thatched
with palm or cocoa-nut leaves.   When we entered this regal hut we found the chief seated near
one end of it, who barely condescended to notice
us as we approached to make our salutations.   We
were not prepared for so rude a reception and felt
somewhat mortified to find a chief of his distinguished rank so totally destitute of courtesy.   We
thought at least that he would have risen from
his sitting posture, and expected more from him
than our after experience taught us we had a right
to look for from people in a state of nature.   The
only furniture in the hut was a few coarse mats.
At one side of it five muskets, highly polished,
were arranged one above the other, over which
hung two kegs of powder sewed up in canvass,
and near them a few long spears and a war conch,
ornamented with human hair.   We made ourselves as much at home as if we had received a
more cordial welcome, and indulged our curiosity
in examining whatever we saw, when suddenly
the chief rose and his silence and gravity were at
once explained.   We had remarked that he had
an uncommonly large black robe thrown over
him, but without the least suspicion that it covered

any one else than himself. He suddenly threw it aside as we came near him and there stood his wife, a girl about eighteen years of age, who had just finished making her toilet. He pointed to her with a look of satisfaction, and uttered " Motake," a word we afterwards learned, signified very good, or very well. Although she was naturally a pretty girl, she had made herself a hideous looking object. She had smeared her face all over with a coarse yellow paint, upon which was drawn streaks of black and green, than which nothing could have appeared more disgusting. She assumed a manner and look of affectation, such as may often have been observed in some self-approving beauty, who, conscious of her charms, feels that she is an object of admiration to all around her. When I expressed my disapprobation of her style of ornament, she stared at me with a look of surprise, which seemed to ask what I was saying. I soon gave both her and the chief to understand, by signs ; after which they seemed not so well pleased with themselves or each other ; and when I saw her again in the evening she was without any ornament, and looked all the better for it. While here, two grotesque figures came in and walked up to me with an austere look. They had a profusion of cock's feathers bound circularly round their brows, broad gorgets of wood ornamented with red berries round their necks, shell bracelets and ornaments of polished shell or bone tied above their ancles. Each held in his hand a fan of palmetto. After standing a few moments, keeping their eyes fixed upon me, they began jumping up and down and fanning themselves, applying both hands to the fan. My first feeling was surprise, mingled with curiosity, to know the cause of their strange appearance; but when they had several times repeated their exercise, the scene was altogether so ridiculous that I could not refrain from laughing. They soon afterwards, without even noticing the chief, turned and walked off. After leaving the hut of the chief, I visited a number of others, all of which were nearly alike. In one of them I saw two drums, the only instruments of music that I met with. The largest of them was a hollow log, from three to four feet long, and about a foot and a half in diameter, covered at both ends with shark skin. I asked the owner to play upon it, to which he readily consented, seeming highly flattered with the invitation. He accompanied his voice by thumping his hands and elbows on the drum-head; but the music that he made was intolerable. He beat, however, in very good time, and had evidently a high opinion of his performance.

In the course of our ramble, one of the officers told an Indian, who had joined us, by signs, that he wanted some cocoa-nuts. The good-natured fellow acquiesced without the least hesitation, and to our great astonishment, ran up a tree standing near us, with the activity of a squirrel. The tree was forty or fifty feet high, having but a slight inclination, yet the climbing seemed to occasion him scarcely any exertion. They do not press their bodies against the tree and hitch themselves up as is customary with us, which, in their naked condition, they could not do without injury. They press the bottoms of their feet against the tree, and clinging to it with their hands one above the other, ascend upon all-fours. It did not strike us with less surprise when he had thrown the cocoa-nuts down, to see with what facility he stripped off the hard husks without the aid of any thing but his teeth. For such a thing to have been accomplished by one of us would be found impossible. We afterwards remarked the same practise in other places, and at other islands. It was general except with the old men, who, unless they were very robust, used a sharp-pointed stick of hard wood to remove the husk.

They could not understand our practice of shaking hands. When we extended a hand to one of them as a mark of friendly salutation, they looked as though they would question what was meant by it; and from their manner seemed to think that our object was to feel their skin, which

E

they would always reciprocate by raising up our sleeves and examining very minutely.

On the morning of the 29th of September, which was the last of our remaining in Comptroller's Bay, I made another excursion to the Typee Bay, taking with me the chief of the Happahs, who was very anxious to go. I wondered at this, as the tribes evinced so much dislike to each other; but afterwards saw, in my intercourse with the natives of the South Sea Islands, that uncivilized men are capable of as much duplicity towards each other as the educated and refined. When we had arrived within a hundred yards of the shore we were met by the chief with whom I had formed an acquaintance on the preceding day. He saluted the chief of the Happahs in a way that indicated a former acquaintance, but with a look and manner somewhat formal. The Typee chief immediately spoke to some one near him, who ran off and in a few minutes returned with a calabash filled with a preparation of the bread-fruit, upon which was poured a quantity of milk expressed from a cocoanut. This was offered by the Typee to the Happah chief, and I was also invited to partake of it. I tasted and found it very palatable. The two chiefs seated themselves in the stern of the boat, and made a hearty breakfast, using their fingers instead of spoons. Neither of them seemed very communicative, as only a few words passed between them at this interview. There was also in the boat a young woman belonging to the chief's family, for whom breakfast was brought in the shell of a cocoa-nut, and which was a preparation of the cocoa-nut and bread-fruit, sour and disagreeable to the taste. This, I was informed, is the food upon which the women almost entirely subsist, they being Tabooed from eating whatever is held in high estimation by the men. When the chiefs had finished their repast, the Typee pointed to his hogs, which he had again caused to be brought down upon the beach, saying that he wanted powder or guns for them, but unfortunately I had neither of these valuable articles with which to make an exchange with him, and he would consider nothing else as an equivalent. He sent for several old muskets that were very much out of order, and proposed to go on board with me and have them repaired, making me understand by signs, that he would in return present me with hogs. His anxiety was so great upon this subject, that I found it difficult to put a stop to his solicitations. In the mean time, however, I saw the schooner underway, and dismissing my Typee friends, pulled away for the Happah Bay. When I had approached within half a mile of the Happah village, the schooner was almost out of the harbour, and the chief observing that I was anxious to get on board, proposed jumping into the water and swimming home, to which I readily consented. He then stripped himself of his neck and ear ornaments, which consisted of two white pieces of polished shell and a carved image of bone, and presenting them to me as a token of his regard, plunged into the water, leaving me free to pursue my way to the vessel without the trouble of landing him. Most of the ornaments worn by these people, are of bone or shells, finely polished or rudely carved. They attach a number of them to a piece of cocoa-nut twine, and wear them around their necks, or wrists, or ancles, as may be most agreeable to the taste and fancy of the individuals. A more expensive and difficult ornament to obtain is a gorget. It is a piece of wood, semi-circular, about three inches wide, carved to fit the neck, covered with a beautiful red and black berry, and stuck on with a gum that oozes from the tree of the bread-fruit. On the hill that rises to the left of the valley, we planted a variety of seeds of fruit, vegetables and grain, but the natives of the valley are so totally ignorant of every thing that relates to agriculture, that it is not probable they will ever derive any advantage from them. Whilst we were in Happah Bay, the weather was clear and delightful. The temperature so regular that no change was felt in the transition from day to night.

On the 30th of September, we stood out of Comptroller's Bay, and ran down for Massachusetts' Bay, a place made familiar to our countrymen by Commodore Porter's long and interesting visit. The two points that form the harbours of Comptroller's and Massachusetts' Bays, are about seven miles distant from each other. At one, P. M., we were clear of the projecting southern point of Comptroller's Bay, and at three, P. M., anchored in eight fathoms water, within half a mile of the hill at the bottom of the bay, called Porter's Monument. Before we came to anchor, the water was covered with canoes, and people of both sexes and all ages swimming towards us, and as soon as the vessel lost her head way, they were crawling up on all sides like so many rats. They were not less delighted with our arrival than were the Happahs. Hundreds were collected on the shore, and all expressing their satisfaction by songs and dances. Amongst our first visitors, were two English sailors who had deserted from whale ships, and been long enough resident on the island to converse in the language of the natives. With them came also a native of Nooaheeva, and a native of Otaheite, both of whom had served a considerable time in whale ships, and could converse in broken English. We were therefore in no want of interpreters, and it seemed at once to introduce us to the confidence and friendship of our new acquaintances.

The harbour of Massachusetts' Bay is spacious and affords good anchorage for ships of the largest class. The only part of it, however, where landing is not attended with difficulty and some danger, is the east side, where there is a fine sand beach from a quarter to half a mile long, at one extremity of which empties a small rivulet of pure and excellent water into the bay. Landing may be effected at the watering-place beyond Porter's Monument, where there is a more considerable stream of fresh water, but it is always difficult, and when the surf is high, cannot fail to be dangerous. At this place we watered the Dolphin; but had to swim the casks to and from the shore, and altogether, it was a laborious undertaking. Along the east and north part of the bay there is a long reef that makes at a short distance from the shore, upon which a heavy surf is always breaking. In entering the bay, the whole habitable part of this section of the island is presented at one view, and forms a most grand and beautiful landscape. It is nearly semi-circular, and rises like an amphitheatre, in fruitful and populous circular ranges of hills, until at the distance of several miles, it terminates in a circumference of high and gloomy mountains, the tops of which resemble a massive wall. This rude and barren circle of mountain contrasts finely with the fertile ranges below, covered with their forests of cocoa-nut and bread-fruit trees, and huts and villages every where scattered about through hill and dale. Nor is the extreme elevation without its interest and beauty. A number of little cataracts reflecting the rays of the sun and looking like sheets of liquid silver, break in upon the gloom of the sterile rock, adding brilliancy as they descend to the lively prospect below. After a shower, not less than fifty of these splendid falls of water may be seen, some of which are but just perceptible through the intervening space between hills and trees, producing an effect peculiarly agreeable. What is called Porter's Monument, is a round hill from fifty to an hundred feet high, situated at the east extremity of the bay. It was here that Commodore Porter had his Fort, not a vestige of which is now remaining. It is overrun with a wild luxuriant growth of vines and grass, and no trace of a footstep can be found. On one side of the hill, near its base, was stretched a bark line, which was attended by a man who calls himself Opotee, and who declares the hill beyond it to be tabooed. Upon one occasion, as I was approaching it, some natives called out "Taboo, Taboo!" but Opotee immediately expressed his willingness that I should pass, as I was a countryman of his namesake, Opotee. To the north of Porter's Monument, and back from the sand beach, where was the navy-yard, all is now overgrown with bushes and trees, some of which have attained to a considerable size. Like the monument, there is no indication of its ever having been occupied for any human purpose.

On the first of October, the day after our arrival, I went on shore, taking with me a great variety of seeds, for the purpose of planting them where it was most probable they would be taken care of and come to maturity. The natives flocked round me in great numbers. There was not less than a hundred boys with the crowd of men and women that followed me. They were highly delighted when they discovered my object, which was explained to them by John Luxon, the native of Nooaheeva, who spoke English. Whenever we came to a rough or muddy place, which was frequently the case, the boys and men, notwithstanding my remonstrances, would mount me on their shoulders and carry me over, with loud shouting. I could easily perceive that this was a frolic with those who engaged in it, and done out of levity and the caprice of the moment; but I could not but feel that they had been first stimulated to it by the favourable impression they had conceived of my design. I planted some things in unfrequented places where I found a clear spot, but most of the seeds and fruit-pits, in the enclosures of the natives. John Luxon was a man of some rank as a chief, and possessed considerable property. To one of his enclosures that was large and seemed to have been attended with unusual care, I devoted most of my attention. There, aided by several of the natives, who laboured with great assiduity, I prepared the ground and made quite an extensive plantation of orange, lemon, cheromaya, peach, apricot, water-melons, pumpkins, potatoes, onions, beans, corn, and a variety of other fruits and grain, from Peru. He expressed himself in terms of the warmest gratitude, and I have no doubt that the natives have already experienced the most important benefits from the memento I left them of the Dolphin's visit to their Island.

In the course of my days' occupation, I was several times driven into Luxon's house by the frequent showers that came over. I no sooner entered, than the natives flocked after me, and in a few minutes the hut would be crowded. The little boys and girls here shewed me the same officious attention that I received in making my way to the village, but expressed in a different manner. As many as could approach would surround me with their fans, keeping them going until the rain ceased, and I was again enabled to resume my work. This was a kind of civility, peculiarly agreeable, as the weather was oppressively warm; but I could not fail to discover that my little attendants were all candidates for my friendly notice and bestowed their civility with the expectation of some reward. I had a few trifles about me, but not enough to give to all, and felt at a loss in what way I should make my presents, fearing that the least favoured would be mortified and displeased. It seemed however to make no difference. It was all "motake"* with them. All seemed satisfied. On my return to the beach, I found it thronged with men, women, and children. All the beauty and fashion of Massachusetts' Bay had assembled in honour of our arrival, decked out in their finest tappas, and gayest colours. The females were dressed in the best style of their island, with neat turbans of tappa-cloth, white, or ornamented with colours, a white robe of the same material thrown loosely over them, tastefully knotted on one shoulder, concealing half the bosom, and a wrapper round the waist that reached below the knee. They were arranged in groups of a dozen each, singing merrily and clapping their hands in time to the music of their voices. A little way from them the men were seated in the same manner and similarly occupied. The ladies, to improve their charms, had used an abundant quantity of cocoa-nut oil, which filled the air with its nauseous perfumes for an hundred yards round. Many of them had more highly anointed them-

* Very good, or very well.

selves with yellow paint, which, with the cocoa-
nut oil, was running from them in streams. Some
had decorated themselves with necklaces of a
golden yellow fruit which bears a strong resemblance to a pine-apple, and emits a powerful offensive smell. At a distance, with their variegated
robes flying in the wind, their appearance was
altogether agreeable, and upon a near approach
the scene was animated beyond description. The
dusk of evening was the signal for their disper-
sion, when some went one way and some another.
On the second of October, I wandered back upon
the hills, and had all the boys with me that followed me on the preceding day.

They renewed their frolic of carrying me, and
whenever I seated myself, came round me as
many as could approach, each with a green leaf
for a fan. I entered unceremoniously a number
of the huts, where I almost always found one or
more men, in nearly every instance, extended on
their backs, their heads resting on a log laid along
on one side of the hut, and their heels on another,
about four feet from the first. They would never
rise to receive me, but utter "motake," when I
was perceived by them, and make motions for me
to do as they did, offering me at the same time a
fan, one of which they were using almost constantly. In the course of my ramble, I met with a
little girl, twelve or fourteen years old, who was

very pretty, attended by a servant, the only instance in which I remarked such a thing on the
island. She was evidently walking out to make a
visit, and had just arrived at the house of her
destination when I met her. I put some beads
round her neck, which seemed to delight her very
much ; but an old man present, whose hut she was
about to visit, assumed an angry look, and seemed
to threaten by his manner. He changed his conduct, however, when I made him a trifling present,
and the little girl, taking my hand, led me to her
father's hut. He was a chief of some consequence, as was indicated by the possession of two
or three casks of powder, and six muskets. These
he took down, and displayed very ostentatiously,
and wanted to know if I had not others to dispose
of. His conduct was altogether kind and hospitable, in acknowledgment for which I made him a
present at my departure. Whenever I wanted
cocoa-nuts to quench my thirst, I had only to sig-
nify it to one of the men that was following me
about, and he would supply me from the nearest
tree. With one fellow I was very much amused.
He carried his arms full of cocoa-nuts following
me about nearly all day, and when I returned to
the vessel I presented him with a musket ball,
with which he was perfectly satisfied, said it was
" motake," and went away. When I returned to
the beach in the evening, I found the natives, male

and female, assembled in as great numbers as on
the day previous, and amusing themselves in the
same way. The females were again in their
finest attire, and at a distance might any where
else have been mistaken for an assemblage of
fashionable belles. We were apprehensive that
our men, a number of whom were at work on
shore, would have been very much annoyed by the
intrusion of the natives. This, however, was not
the case. When they commenced their work in
the morning a circle was made, comprehending
the whole space we wished them to occupy, which
we told the natives was tabooed, and there was
not an instance of their passing it. The next day
they held quite a fair on the beach. Amongst
other things, they had for trade large quantities of
cocoa-nuts and bread-fruit. The former they exchanged for small pieces of tobacco; but a piece
of iron hoop, fashioned into a tool or instrument
of husbandry, was demanded for the latter. They
were all day on the beach, cooking and eating
their bread-fruit and cocoa-nuts. In the evening, the boys and men amused us with playing soldiers, by ranging themselves in a line with
sticks for muskets. One of our officers took a
particular pleasure in making grimaces, and talking a gibberish to the natives in imitation of their
manner of speaking. It was very offensive to
them; but they respected us too much to betray

their displeasure. Upon one occasion, however, he amused himself in this way with the boys, about a hundred of whom were assembled, when I encouraged them to retaliate on him, by clucking like a hen. They soon discovered that it was disagreeable to him, and assembled round him like so many little furies, clucking with all their might. It seemed to delight them to have an opportunity of revenging themselves upon him, which they did most amply, for they did not let him rest a moment until he went on board, which was soon afterwards, highly displeased with me for conspiring with the Indians against him. We were often amused with the strange and ridiculous taste of the natives in the article of dress.

They were all desirous of obtaining clothes, and a number of old garments were given them, or exchanged for curiosities by the officers and crew. When obtained, whether they fitted or not, the Indians immediately put them on, and scarcely ever more than one garment at a time. Thus, half naked and half attired, a native would walk about with exceeding gravity, admiring himself, and believing that every one else was equally pleased with his genteel appearance.

Whenever they seated themselves to sing, a person was selected to occupy a conspicuous station, and perform a dance round the circle, slowly, and in the most graceful native style, striking at the same time the hollow of his left arm with his right hand, in time with the music of their voices. This distinction was always conferred upon some one who had obtained an old jacket or tattered shirt. If he had on a jacket, it was sure to be buttoned closely round him, with the two or three remaining buttons, and the sleeves, if not torn off, would probably not reach more than half the length of his arms. Thus attired, he would perform his evolutions round the circle slowly, and with a most serious air, stopping occasionally to receive the applause of the singers, who bestowed it upon him with great enthusiasm. Soon after daylight, one morning I was on the beach, and my curiosity led me to a place, where a number of females were busily employed in collecting something from the rocks. When I approached them they discontinued their occupation, and would have fled, but I called them back, and prevailed upon them to renew their occupation. Each of them was provided with a green leaf, in which she was gathering from the rocks a species of fine green sea moss and small snails. What they preserved in the leaf was intended for their families at home. They ate freely of them, and said it was "motake." The moss was tender, but to me had no other taste than that of salt water, with which it was covered at high tide. The snails were not larger than a pea, covered with a hard shell, and when broken, heated the tongue like pepper. The moss, when gathered, had a most disgusting appearance. I was told by the Englishmen, residing here, that the natives esteem it a very great delicacy. One of the females had an infant with her a few months old, which she was teaching to swim by holding it in a pool of water, and occasionally letting it go. The infant would make a slight effort, when let go by the mother, and, no doubt, was taught to swim almost as soon as it could walk. On the third of October, in walking through the habitable part of the valley, I was every where met by females, who addressed me with a smile, and finely modulated tone of voice, " Coare ta whyhene?" * The father of one of these, good naturedly conducted me to the hut of a chief, highest in blood of any in the valley. He was a man upwards of fifty, and apparently more civilized than any of the natives I had seen before. He told the interpreter to say, that he felt pleasure in seeing me at his hut. It was about forty by twenty feet, and constructed in the same way as that occupied by the Happah chief, differing in no respect from those of the common people, except in dimensions. His rank and importance was displayed in the possession of six muskets, and two casks of powder that hung directly fronting the door, and which the chief took occasion to point out to me soon after

* Don't you want a wife?

I entered. To him they were a treasure, and, in fact, the wealth and consequence of every individual seemed to be estimated by this standard alone. The powder was covered over with canvass, and the muskets highly polished. On one side of the hut were two logs, about three feet apart, and between them a coarse mat, for the convenience of laying down on, one log being intended for the head, and the other for the feet. Whilst I was here, a number of visiters came in, and, walking directly to the logs, without noticing any one, threw themselves down between them, their heads on one, and feet on the other, where they lay, fanning themselves, and looking at us, without saying a word, except once or twice, when they saw me looking at them, I was saluted with "motake." In the middle of the hut was the coffin of the chief's father, who had died about six months previous. It was the trunk of a large bread-fruit tree, six or eight feet long, highly polished, and the lid so ingeniously fitted, that the place of contact could not be seen but by the closest examination. He told me that his father had been a great warrior, and the friend of Opotee.* Before his door was a swivel, and a number of shot, that he said he had obtained from Opotee. He prized them very highly, although they could not be of the least use to him, except as they served to gratify

F   * Com. Porter.

his vanity. When I expressed a desire to know the manner in which they prepared the paint, used by the females, he directed his son to get some of the root, and grind it between two stones, mixing a little water with it, the only process required. I gave the chief's wife (who was an old woman) some beads, and a cotton handkerchief, with which she was so delighted, that she threw both her arms around my neck, and embraced me most affectionately. She was painted all over, quite yellow, and so thoroughly smeared my clothes, that I paid dearly for this expression of her regard. At parting, the chief presented me with a hog (the only one we obtained at the Marquesas), some sticks of the tappa tree, and offered whatever was acceptable to me, about his house. We also exchanged names, and I promised again to visit him, but had no opportunity afterwards. His son accompanied me on board, carrying the presents his father had made me, and all the way calling me " Kappe," the name of his father, and himself, by my name.

In the evening, when I returned to the vessel, she was crowded with natives, the work of the day being completed. The men and women were in different circles, singing their songs. That of the women, resembled the croaking of a great many frogs. The quick and lively motion of their hands, accompanying the various modulations of the voice, exhibited a great activity, and command of muscle, and was far more pleasing than their music. There was one amongst the females, who possessed great powers of voice, in the utterance of strange sounds, in which none of the rest could accompany her. The performance seemed to distress her very much, and was certainly very disagreeable; yet the natives would all stop occasionally, to listen to her, and, when she was done, exclaimed, with seeming surprise, "motake!"

On the 4th of October, I took a boat, prepared with arms, and providing myself with a few presents, ran down for Lewis' Bay, to ascertain the depth of water at the entrance of the harbour, what difficulties might probably attend our running in with the schooner, and whether it afforded any better prospect than the other places we had visited, of obtaining a supply of hogs. The distance was only six miles, and, with a fine breeze, we were at the entrance of the harbour in little more than an hour. It was very narrow, formed by two high points of land, and the depth of water abundantly sufficient for ships of the largest class. A heavy and broken swell made the entrance appear difficult: and, without a fair wind, it is so confined, that it would be hazardous to attempt it; but the gorge being once passed, you enter a large smooth basin, where there is scarcely a ripple, the land rising high all around it, and the points locking with each other. In the basin we found good anchorage, in from four to nine fathoms water, and a clay bottom. Lewis' Bay is divided into two parts by a projecting point of rocks. I first landed in that which fronts the entrance, or rather went into the edge of the surf. A great many people, of all ages, came swimming off through the surf, and in a few moments the boat was full of them, and of fruit of various kinds. They were anxious for me to land, but I saw there would be great difficulty in my getting off again, in the event of any misunderstanding with them, which was not altogether impossible. I did not remain long, but, dismissing the natives who had crawled into the boat, or were hanging on the gunwale, pulled round the point of rocks to the other landing. When first I went into this part of the harbour, I could perceive only two or three persons, who were afraid to come near us. They gradually relaxed in their timidity, however, and kept nearing us a little, until we at last prevailed upon them to get into the boat. As soon as they saw our muskets, which they thought were intended for trade ; but which were only for our protection, they ran away, saying, they would bring us hogs directly. In the mean time the news of our arrival spread, far and wide, over the valley, and the people came running from every direction, with whatever they could most readily possess themselves of, for trade. Every body wanted muskets, and a chief had seven or eight hogs brought to the beach, all of which he offered for one gun. After spending an hour or two here, on the most friendly terms with the natives, I prepared to depart, and missed one of my shoes, that I had thrown off wet. Search was made in the boat, without finding it, when it was remarked, that a native had been seen crawling in the water for a considerable distance to a rock near the shore, where he deposited something, and returned. Upon examination, we found the shoe wrapped up in a piece of tappa cloth, the Indian having stolen it, without reflecting that the possession of one shoe, without the other, was of no value to him, or perhaps not caring whether it was or not, so that he gratified his propensity to steal. When I returned a short distance, and held the shoe up to show the natives that I had recovered it, they set up a loud laugh, which I interpreted into applause, of the ingenious exploit of their countryman. The valley of Lewis' Bay is not to be compared to either of the other places we visited on the island, for beauty or fertility. It is, however, quite populous, and the scenery is grand and picturesque. The land gradually rises from a small plain below, like the valley occupied by the Typees, in a succession of hills, and terminates in a perpendicular high ledge of rocks. In returning from Lewis' to Massachusetts' Bay, the wind was ahead, and we pulled close in with the shore, which, for nearly the whole distance, rises abruptly, from the ocean, to the height of six or seven hundred feet. Numerous falls, which were only perceptible in heavy mist, before they reached the water, were leaping from the top, whilst the sea beat the sides with unceasing fury, throwing its spray to the height of more than a hundred feet. Whilst we were tugging at our oars, contemplating this magnificent scene, the sea suddenly became unusually agitated, and threatened, at every instant, to swallow up the boat. We pulled directly from the shore, and for half an hour our situation was very critical, after which the sea became regular. A phenomenon, so remarkable, baffled all our speculation, and we were entirely at a loss to determine respecting its cause. On our arrival on board, we learned that the vessel had narrowly escaped being driven on shore in a squall. It was not the fault of the anchorage, but in consequence of the baffling winds which had several times driven the vessel over her anchor, whereby it was fouled by the cable, and tripped with the violence of the squall.

The natives, as usual, were assembled on the shore near us, amusing themselves in their customary way, by singing and dancing. The females, having learned from some of the Dolphin's

crew, that it was not in good taste to use cocoa-
nut oil, and paint, in such profusion, left it off, as
well as the golden yellow fruit, which had also
been highly disapproved of. It improved their
appearance, and they seemed to be sensible of
the superior estimation in which they were held.
These wild ladies, in truth, who, on our first arrival, came swimming round, like so many mer-
maids, grew very fastidious in the short time we
remained at their island. After the first day or
two, they requested to be allowed to go on board,
in our boats, and then, seeing some of the officers
carried through the surf by the seamen, nothing
less would please them, when they did us the
honour of a visit, but to be gallanted on board with
the same ceremony. Our sailors gallantly condescended to gratify two or three of them ; but,
instead of taking them to the boat, they most un-
courteously let them fall into the first heavy roller
they encountered, leaving them to the choice
of swimming to the boat, or back to the shore
again, after which none ever asked to be carried.
With regard to their superstitions or worship, we
could learn but little. John Luxon told me, that
he was tabooed by his father, who was a chief, and
that no common man dared to pass over his head.
He was usually dressed in a sailor's shirt and
trowsers, and an old hat. He came off regularly
every morning, and ate with us three time a day,

taking his seat at the table, without the least ceremony, and never waiting to be asked.

One day, some one had, designedly or accidentally, thrown some bread in John's hat, which he did not perceive when he took it up, and put it on. When he felt the bread upon his head, he threw his hat off instantly, and, with a look of the utmost horror, exclaimed, "who put dat dare? Me Taboo here!" (putting his hand on his head) " To-morrow me sick, me die!" This, he repeated over a number of times, and with great earnestness of manner tried to find out who had put the bread in his hat, insisting upon it, that, on the morrow, he should sicken and die. The morrow, however, came, and John was alive and well, and was heartily laughed at for his foolish superstition, when he came on board as usual to spend the day with us. I do not believe that John had the same implicit faith in taboo afterwards. I tried to find out from him what was meant by his being tabooed, but he spoke English so badly, and seemed to understand so little of the matter himself, that I was not much the wiser for his explanation. We were told here, that, a few years since, the missionaries at the Society Islands, moved by the benevolent purpose of converting the Marquesas islanders to Christianity,. sent one of their number to reside at Massachusetts' Bay. The missionary landed amongst his charge, by

whom he was received with characteristic kindness and hospitality. No other notice was taken
of him, however, than would have been bestowed
upon the most poor and ignorant mariner, seeking
an asylum amongst them. He was permitted to
fix upon his place of residence, and live in such
way as pleased him best. He soon commenced
preaching the doctrines of his faith. The natives
listened to him, wondering at all he said, but not
less at his singular manner of life,—to them
unexampled, in all their acquaintance with the
whites,—and, certainly, unparalleled amongst
themselves. They had always seen the white
men, who visited their islands, take liberties with
their females, and mingle with them in all their
pleasures, whilst this man, who called himself a
messenger from the Great Spirit, lived a life of
celibacy, retired from all that, to them, was amusing or agreeable. When a free interchange of
opinion had taken place amongst them, respecting
him, they came to the conclusion, that he was dif-
ferently made and constituted from all other men
they had ever seen, and curiosity being raised to
the highest pitch, they, with a levity peculiar to
savages, determined to subject him to a scrutiny.
The missionary, alarmed at a disposition that
evinced so little respect for his character and personal rights, took his departure by the first op-

portunity, since which no attempt has been made to convert the natives of the Marquesas to Christianity.

The men of the Marquesas, were, in general, quite naked. But few ornaments were worn by either sex. The women frequently had no other ornament than a small flower, stuck through a slit in their ears. Some of the men wore polished whale's teeth round their necks, and some shell bracelets, but they were not in common use. A few were tattooed all over, and others but slightly. The mode of their tattooing seemed to be altogether a matter of fancy. Some had indulged the most whimsical taste, in having indelibly pricked into their flesh, fish, birds, and beasts, of all kinds known to them. Others were tattooed black, even to the inner part of their lips. It is an art in high estimation amongst them. There are men, who pursue it as a regular business, and are in great favour with their countrymen, for their skilful performance. The women tattoo more tastefully than the men. Their feet and legs, half-way to the knee, are usually covered with figures, wrought with great neatness, and the right hand and arm, half-way to the elbow, is often similarly ornamented. Both men and women commonly wear their hair short, and when instances to the contrary are met with, the persons invariably have a disgusting appearance, their hair hanging in long and disagreeable looking matted locks.

The men are finely formed, large, and active; and both men and women would, in many instances, be considered handsome, were it not for our fastidious objection to their copper colour. Their teeth are very beautiful, and formed a subject of remark to us all, while we were amongst them. I do not think that, of all the people that came under my observation at Nooaheeva, there was a single one with bad teeth. This is the more remarkable in the men, as they are accustomed all their lives to strip the husk of the cocoa-nut in the manner I have described.

A plurality of wives is not admitted amongst them under any circumstances. The sexes rarely live together, as man and wife, until they have arrived at the middle age of life. When a man wishes to take a wife, he first obtains the consent of the female, who solicits that of her friends, which, being obtained, the girl's father kills a hog, or, if a chief, a number of hogs, and makes a feast, to which all the friends of both parties are invited. After this ceremonial is performed, which is an occasion of great merriment, the parents of the girl furnish her with a few pieces of tappa cloth, and she is conducted by her husband to his house. The females, although invited to these feasts, are not permitted to partake of the hogs, roasted for the occasion. They are tabooed for the men alone. Hogs are scarcely ever used by the natives, but upon the occasion of a death or marriage. When a chief, or other person dies, possessing many hogs, a great feast is made. The only arms, that are now generally used, are muskets. Most of the natives, who have any property, own one or more. I did not see a single war club at Nooaheeva, and but few spears. I met several persons, who had the scars of musket balls, that they told me were received in battle. Each of the renegade Englishmen was living with a chief, who thought there was scarcely any thing that he could not perform. Besides supporting them, they gave them all the consequence of chiefs in their intercourse with the natives, so far as their own authority would admit of it. They were highly respected by the natives, and even John Luxon boasted to me of his superiority over the other Indians, in speaking English. I asked John, of what advantage his speaking English was to him, to which he replied, that it enabled him to cheat his countrymen.

The whole face of the island of Nooaheeva is high and mountainous. Every part I visited is composed of volcanic cinders, and evidently owes its origin to some great convulsion of nature. Whilst we remained at Massachusetts' Bay, the

weather was mild and pleasant. We had several
heavy showers, which, in one instance, only was
accompanied with a squall of wind. After these
showers it was delightful to contemplate the beauty
of the innumerable little cascades of water every
where falling over the rocks from the tops of the
mountains. In a few hours, many of them would
become less brilliant, and some would quite disap-
pear. We found the longitude of our anchorage
by the mean of three chronometers, to be one hundred and thirty-nine degrees fifty-four minutes
and thirty seconds west; latitude, by a series of
observations, eight degrees fifty-seven minutes
forty-five seconds south.

October the 5th, we got under way, and stood
out with a light and baffling wind, tacking very
close in with both shores. At nine, A.M., we passed
the Sentinels, and bore up to the westward with a
moderate breeze from E. S. E. The islands Rooahooga and Rooapooa, were plainly in sight. In
clear weather they may be seen at least fifty
miles. The amiable character of the inhabitants
of Nooaheeva, and the friendly disposition they
had evinced towards us upon all occasions, made
us feel regret at leaving them so soon. The
course that now lay before us, carried us away
from all the civilized world; and the islands in
our way affording but little to tempt navigators to
visit them, were known to us only as places, ex-

isting on the wide surface of the ocean, where, with few exceptions, the inhabitants had never seen the face of a white man. We could anticipate no other gratification from our contemplated visit to them, than the indulgence of our curiosity. The weather became squally after our departure from the Marquesas, and continued so for several days, during which time we were frequently deceived by the clouds assuming the strongest appearance of land, for which we steered two or three times, under a full conviction that we had made a discovery. We could picture to ourselves, the mountains, and valleys, and bays, and, to confirm the deception, we frequently saw land birds flying about us.

At day-light, on the 10th of October, we discovered Caroline Island, bearing W. S. W, and distant fourteen miles. We were on the weather side of it, and a furious surf was every where in sight, breaking upon a reef some distance from the shore. We stood along to the westward, and at nine, A.M., passed a reef, that makes out from the N. W. end of the island, protecting it to the S. W. from the heavy easterly swell, and prevailing winds. Under the lee of the reef, we stood in, with the hope of finding anchorage, getting frequent casts of the lead, until, to our great disappointment, it was discovered that there was deep sea-water within a few feet of a bed of coral,

that stretched off three or four hundred yards
from the shore. Farther to the south and west, a
high surf was breaking, and this being the only
place where we could land, and, desirous of exploring the island, we took a small kedge to the
coral bank, by which we rode to the easterly trade
winds. Here we landed without much difficulty,
and made our way to the shore, over the coral,
although it was full of holes, and looked as though
it would give way under our feet. The holes in
the coral-bed were from one to three feet deep,
and some of them had the appearance of commu-
nicating with the ocean. In these holes, we found
an abundance of large and very fine fish, with
which we supplied the crew in great plenty. They
were of several different kinds, the best of which
were the red grouper, and a long fish, of a dark
colour, for which we had no name. Boarding
pikes and boat-hooks were the only instruments
we used for taking them, and by this simple ap-
paratus alone a frigate's crew might have been
supplied in a short time. A boat was also sent
to fish alongside of the coral bank, where were
myriads of red grouper, of a large size; but the
sharks were so numerous, that, for every fish, we
lost two or three hooks.

The tide rises, at Caroline Island, from three to
four feet, and, at low water, the coral-bank was
nearly dry. This was the case when we landed,

and, having remained there several hours, our
fishing party was surprised with a rise of the
water, that made it difficult, and somewhat dangerous for them to retrace their steps to the edge
of the bank, the holes in many places not being
perceptible, and the water in them over their
heads.   What made their situation the more disagreeable was the number of sharks that had
come in with the tide, and which occasionally
made a bite at their feet or legs.   One man, who
had a large bunch of fish which he trailed through
the water, was so closely pursued, and fiercely
attacked by them, that he was compelled to take
refuge upon a rock that lay in his way, from
which he could not again be prevailed upon to
descend, until the boat went to his relief.   Caroline Island is uninhabited.   It is from five to eight
miles long, and no where in the vicinity of our
anchorage more than from a quarter to half a
mile wide.   There are some trees of a large size
upon it, and in most places a thick growth of underwood.   It is every where bounded by a bed of
coral, which generally extends several hundred
yards from the shore.   We saw no animals on it,
and no other reptiles than small lizards.   Sea
birds were tolerably numerous, and a few sand
snipe were seen.   On the weather side of the
island, we found a cocoa-nut tree, that, to all
appearance, had but recently drifted on shore.

Besides the cocoa-nut tree, we found two articles of Indian furniture. That they came from an inhabited island, there can be no doubt, and it is equally certain that the island has never been discovered, as there is none laid down upon the chart, in the direction of the trade winds, from Caroline Island, nearer than the Society Islands. The Marquesas are the nearest to Caroline, of any land known; and they are distant upwards of six hundred miles, and differ in their bearing a little from the general direction of the trade winds. On the cocoa-nut tree there were two nuts, which had the appearance of having been but a short time in the water. We planted them near our anchorage. Caroline Island is low, and every where flat, with the exception of a few sand hillocks, that rise a little above the ordinary level. It is no where more than four or five feet above the sea. We obtained a boat-load of pepper-grass and pursely, of which there was a great abundance; and on the 13th, at meridian, unhooked our kedge, and made sail to the westward. Our place of landing at Caroline Island, was south latitude nine degrees fifty-four minutes thirty seconds; west longitude, one hundred and fifty degrees eighteen seconds.

Previous to taking our departure from the coast of Peru, the commander of the station had furnished us with a long list of islands, said to have

G

been recently discovered by whalers, and we were now in the vicinity of two of them, one of which was laid down in south latitude eight degrees forty minutes; and west longitude one hundred and fifty-nine degrees fifty minutes. The other, in south latitude, six degrees forty-two minutes; west longitude one hundred and sixty-six degrees ten minutes. After our departure from Caroline Island, we steered for the supposed new discovery, that was nearest to us, being that in latitude eight degrees forty seconds; and, having cruised two days in the vicinity, bore away, under a full conviction that it did not exist, or had been laid down incorrectly. In our search for the other island, we were equally unsuccessful; and after running down a degree or two of longitude, in its parallel of latitude, continued on to the southward and westward, shaping our course for the Duke of Clarence Island. Whilst we were looking for these new discoveries, we were frequently deceived by the same false appearance of land, that I have noticed soon after our departure from the Marquesas, and several times we saw land-birds* flying about the vessel.

At four, A. M., on the 29th of October, we dis-

---

* A bird commonly called the sand-snipe. We afterwards saw them so frequently at sea, where no land was known to exist, that their presence produced no other interest than would have arisen from the appearance of a gull, or any other aquatic bird.

covered the Duke of Clarence Island ahead, twelve miles from us. At day-light, the N. W. end was full in sight, and on each side of it, apparently at a great distance, the tops of the trees could but just be seen through the haze of the morning, looking as though they rose from the ocean. As we approached nearer, a great many islets rose to view, connected with each other by a chain of coral reefs. In sailing round them, we discovered that they formed a polygon, the sides of which were narrow strips of land and coral reefs, comprehending within them a lake of many miles in circumference. When we first got close in with the island, this lake, intervening between us and the most distant islets that rose at the utmost limit of our vision, almost persuaded us, for a time, that it was an extensive group, instead of one little island that looked like a speck upon the general chart. The lake was everywhere protected against the ocean, and so smooth, that not an undulation could be seen upon its surface. The wind was light, the sea smooth,—the air had the mildness and elasticity of a spring morning; and these deep green spots, upon the wide waste of ocean, were truly beautiful. The islets were low, rising but a few feet above the water, and all covered with a thick growth of cocoa-nut trees. When we run down within a few miles of the shore to the westward, where, near the beach, were a few huts, two canoes put off, and pulled for us with great rapidity, and shortly afterwards not less than twenty were in sight.

All this part of the shore was bounded by a coral reef, upon which was breaking a heavy surf, and as we wished to anchor, and look for water, we continued on for the leeward shore. We were under easy sail, and the canoes kept way with us, constantly increasing in number, having, each of them, from four to seven men. One of them came very near us, and to save the natives the labour of working at their paddles, we threw them the end of a rope. They laid hold of it very eagerly, but instead of tying it to some part of their canoe, as we expected they would have done, they hauled up by it as close to our stern as they could get, and made motions for us to give them more. We did so, and they again motioned us to veer to. This, we thought unnecessary, as they had already sufficient for the purpose we intended. When they found that their solicitations for more were not heeded, they very deliberately took a sharp instrument of bone or shell, and cut the rope off, having several fathoms in their canoe. As soon as they had done this, they took to their paddles, and pulled away for us with all their might, and were soon again near enough to have a rope thrown to them, which they called for as loud as they could, making, at the same time, significant motions. When they found that we would not give them the rope again, they paddled up to our quarter, and one of them, who was a powerful man, came on board, without seeming to fear us in the least. Several of the officers spoke to him, and tried to call his attention; but, without taking the least notice of any body, he walked straight to the stern-netting, where he commenced most industriously to throw into his canoe every thing that he could lay hands on. The quarter-master and others, who were near, remonstrated with him, in vain, against such outrageous conduct. Their interference seemed only to excite his indignation, and make him the more active in accomplishing his design. When we found that nothing else would prevail with him, I took a musket that lay near me, and gave him a slight blow with it, calling at the same time on some of the men, who stood near, to lay hold of him. He seized the musket, when I struck him, and would have taken me overboard with it, but for the timely assistance of those who were near. He made his escape before the men could get hold of him, having succeeded in throwing into his canoe the log-reel and line, besides a number of other articles, that we could not conveniently spare. We would have pursued the canoe, and taken from it the stolen articles, but they all moved with such rapidity, that we had no hope of overtaking them, if we made the attempt. When the natives in the other canoes had witnessed the success of their comrades in carrying off their booty, which they were displaying to those around them, with great delight, they were encouraged to come near, and make a similar attempt at plunder. They were somewhat cautious, however, having witnessed the resistance we made. The next theft was that of breaking off one of the rudder-irons of the waist-boat. The captain, who was near, prevailed upon the fellow to give it up, which he did, without the least hesitation; but, remaining quietly where he was, he seized the opportunity, when the captain's face was turned from him, and, snatching the piece of iron out of his hands, jumped overboard, and swam to the nearest canoe. We were all the time close in with the shore, getting frequent casts of the deep sea lead, and the moment it was overboard, and the line was seen by the natives, they made for it in a dozen canoes, and with instruments of sharp shells, fastened to sticks, endeavoured to cut it off. They paid not the slightest attention to our remonstrances and threats, and the only way in which we could prevent them from effecting their object, was by hauling the line in as fast as possible.

After running along the shore for several miles, seeking in vain for anchorage, we began to exa-

mine the reefs, that connected the islets, with
great solicitude, in the hope of finding an opening
into the lake, where we should be protected from
the wind and sea. Of this, however, we soon
despaired, and passing the south-west point of the
island, a beautiful little bay opened to our view,
upon the shore of which the surf beat less violently than we had seen it elsewhere. Here we
hove to, and sent a boat in shore to look for anchorage. She soon returned with a report that,
within less than half a cable's length of the shore,
no bottom could be found, with upwards of a hundred fathoms of line. We now gave up all intention of anchoring, and permitted the natives to
come alongside, and exchange whatever we had,
that was mutually acceptable to each other. They
had continued to follow us, and, growing bold
with their numbers, frequently threw on board of
the vessel clubs, cocoa-nuts, or whatever they had
in their canoes, that could be used as missiles.
This was accompanied by such a loud shouting,
and they had become so numerous, that the orders
for the ordinary duty of the vessel could not be
heard. Some of their clubs were so large, as to
be capable of inflicting a fatal blow by the violence with which they were thrown, and our ap-
prehensions of suffering some evil consequence
from this licentious conduct of our new acquaintances, were soon realised, by one of them strik-

ing the surgeon upon the head. He was in ill
health, and had just come upon deck to witness
the novel spectacle around us, when the unwel-
come salutation was given. It alarmed us at first
for his safety; but, to our gratification, we discovered that his hat had so far protected his head,
that the wound was not severe. As soon as the
natives saw the schooner heave to, they closed
around us, and as many as could get alongside,
came with whatever they had to offer. Nearly a
hundred canoes were assembled, and in them
several hundred men. When they saw us hoist-
ing out our boat for the purpose of sounding, they
became alarmed, and took to flight. No inducement could prevail upon them to come near us,
whilst the boat lay alongside, and as soon as she
shoved off, they took to their paddles, and retreated as fast as they could; but when they saw
that she took a different direction, and it was not
her object to pursue them, they all turned and
followed her. They gathered around her at a
short distance, apparently afraid to approach
nearer, at first making signs for her to go on
shore, where was a numerous group of men,
women, and children, inviting our people to land.
Seeing that the boat would not go on shore, and
after the duty assigned had been accomplished,
that she was returning to the schooner, the natives
with one accord closed more nearly around her,

as if to intercept her passage.   The officer in the
boat made threats and signs for them to retire, to
which they paid not the slightest attention.   A
canoe came on each side of the boat, and the natives laid hold of the oars, a man rising in each
canoe at the same time, with a barbed spear,
which he held in the attitude of throwing.   The
officer, feeling that his situation was a very critical one, and thinking that the report of his pocket
pistol would cause them to desist, presented it
with a design to fire ahead of one of the canoes.
It did not go off, but the snap was a signal sufficient for our men to prepare for their defence,
believing they were exposed to the greatest danger.   They seized their pistols, with one of which
each man was provided, and before the officer
could interfere to prevent them from firing (the
noise and confusion amongst the natives being
such, that he could not be heard) one of the men
discharged his piece, and the ball passed through
the hand of one of the natives.   They became
alarmed at the extraordinary report of the pistol,
and immediately after it, seeing the blood flow
from the hand of their countryman, discontinued
their assault, and retired with precipitation.   The
boat then returned to the schooner unmolested,
the natives flying from her in every direction as
she approached them.   We were apprehensive
that the report of the pistol, and the wounding one

of the natives would produce so great a panic
amongst them, as to interrupt our farther intercourse. But in this we were agreeably disappointed, for the boat was no sooner hoisted in,
than they came alongside, with as much confidence, as though nothing of the kind had occurred. In an hour afterwards, the wounded man
was seen in a canoe, fifty or a hundred yards
from us, apparently afraid to come nearer. He
was distinguished by having his hand bound up in
green leaves. After making motions to him, and
those around us, and holding up a variety of
things for his acceptance, he was at last prevailed
upon to come near us. When he saw the sentinel,
in the gangway, he stopped, and we in vain held
up our presents for him, until the sentinel was
removed. He then came on board, and suffered
his wound to be examined and dressed, trembling
and staring around him, like one in the greatest
terror. We were gratified to find that the wound
was not so severe as was to have been apprehended, the ball having passed through the fleshy
part of his hand, between the thumb and fore-
finger, without breaking any bones, and probably
without inflicting upon him a serious injury. When
his wound was dressed, and he received a few
presents of old iron, &c., to him invaluable, he
left us, and jumped from one canoe to another,
with the activity of a monkey, holding up his

treasure, and talking with great vehemence, apparently delighted with his good fortune. The natives had nothing to exchange with us but a few mats, some of which were finely wrought, cocoanuts, bone and shell ornaments, and fishing-hooks, for which we gave them, in return, pieces of iron hoops, or old nails. We witnessed several instances of dishonesty amongst them, as well as their entire want of confidence in us. Whenever one of them presented any thing for exchange, he held it firmly grasped in his hand, until he received his pay with the other ; and if he first obtained the old nail or iron hoop, without the person, with whom he was trading, getting firmly hold of his mat or whatever it might be, he was sure to keep both. Every man carried a long spear, and some of them a short weapon, slightly curved like a sword. Their spears were from eight to twelve feet long, some of which had one and some two branches near the end. They were pointed with the hard bone of a large fish, and, from one to two feet from the point, covered with rows of shark's teeth, that were immoveably fixed by a neat moulding of twine passing through the teeth, and round the spear. The short weapons were armed in the same manner all over, except a small part left for the grasp of the hand. Both were formidable weapons, and capable of

inflicting a mortal wound. A few of them wore
dry wreaths of cocoa-nut leaves round their brows,
which were the only kind of covering we saw any
of them have about their heads, and as the instances were rare, we thought it probable that
they were chiefs. The dress for their loins consisted of two pieces, one of which was composed
of a few plaited leaves, next to the skin, and the
other consisted of a mat, from two to three feet
wide, and four long, beautifully fringed at the
bottom, and which served, not only as a pretty
ornament, but was useful as a protection against
the flies, which almost everywhere amongst these
islands are very troublesome. They were strong
and robust looking men, of a very dark copper
colour, and most of them, particularly the old men,
covered with scars, that they gave us to understand were occasioned by wounds from their
spears and daggers. They wore their hair long,
and in disagreeable looking matted locks. None
of them had heavy beards, and in general but
little. It is not improbable that they pull them
out with fish-scales, as is practised at the Marquesas, and many others of the South Sea Islands.
This is done by compressing the beard with the
fingers between two large fish-scales, in the manner of applying a pair of tweezers. A great
many natives, most of them women and children,

had assembled on the shore, opposite to us, where they remained all day, singing and amusing themselves. No females came off in the canoes.

We saw no water, except a small quantity that one or two of the natives had in cocoa-nut shells, and, much to our regret, from ignorance of their language, could not inquire where it was to be obtained. The land no where rose more than from three to seven feet above the level of the sea, and as we could not land with safety, we had no means of ascertaining whether any rivulets existed upon it. The island seemed to produce nothing, but cocoa-nuts, which must be the only food of the natives, except when they are so fortunate as to catch fish. Towards evening we stood out of the bay, and hove to off the south-west point, where we sent a party on shore to collect a quantity of cocoa-nuts, of which there was a dense forest, that promised an abundant supply. Our people were no sooner on shore than they saw the natives approaching them in different directions, armed with spears and paddles, making signals to each other, and signs, for the intruders to depart. Every tree had some peculiar mark, from whence we concluded, it was considered the property of some individual. It was after sun-down, and night was closing in fast upon our party, who finding, from the determined manner of the natives, that, whatever they took, must be by violence, gave up the enterprise, and returned to the beach. It was fortunate that they did so, for the tide had risen considerably, and with it the surf had increased in a dangerous degree. All, however, got off safe, but with wet jackets, and at eight, P. M., October the 30th, we hoisted in the boat, and made sail.

We ran off with a fine breeze, and at half-past three, A. M., made the Duke of York's Island, directly ahead, and sooner than we expected. It was not more than three or four miles off; the deep hollow roar of the surf could be distinctly heard, and its foaming white crest seen through the mists of the night, as it tumbled on the shore. We hove to until morning, when we made sail along the land, towards the south end of the island. This island is noted on the chart, as uninhabited, when discovered by Commodore Byron, in 1791; and it may be supposed, that we were not a little surprised, on approaching the southern point, to see two canoes putting off for us. One of them came alongside, the other kept at a distance. The first had but one man in it, who exchanged a mat for a piece of iron hoop, and returned immediately to the shore, followed by his consort. When we got to the southward of the point, which was the lee side of the island, we hove to, and sent a boat to look for anchorage. The shores were similar to those of Caroline and Clarence Islands,—of coral, and shelving suddenly into deep sea-water. It was somewhat better here, however, for within half a cable's length of the surf, we let go our anchor in twenty fathoms water. Although we veered eighty fathoms of cable, the bottom was so smooth, and its angle of depression so great, that we drifted off.

We stood in again, and running the vessel close in with the edge of the surf (the wind blowing off shore) came to in eight fathoms. In a few minutes, a native made his appearance on the coral bank, near us, with his arms full of cocoa-nuts, which he held up, as if for our acceptance, waving at the same time a green branch, and frequently jumping about upon the rocks, in a childish, playful manner. A boat was sent to bring him off; but when he saw her approaching pretty near, he threw the nuts in the water towards her, and hastily retired. A coral bed, like that at Caroline Island, extended off fifty or a hundred yards from the shore, which, like that, was perforated every where with holes, and resembled, in its frail appearance, ice that has been for a long time exposed to rain. The tide was low, and the surf breaking but lightly upon it, we were enabled to land without difficulty. At our approach the natives all ran off, and for a considerable time could not be prevailed upon to come near us. After a while their timidity relaxed, and they came round

us, one by one, until we had a dozen of them
assembled. Still they were very much afraid,
starting with every motion we made, and if we
attempted to touch them, they ran from us, and
became as shy as ever. From our place of landing, we could discover that this island was similar
to the Duke of Clarence, being a narrow chain of
little islets and reefs, of coral formation, covered
with bushes and cocoa-nut trees, and comprehending within the chain a lake of many miles in circumference.

At our place of landing, the island between the
ocean and inland sea, was not more than two
hundred yards wide, and this appeared to be as
wide as any part of the chain that came under
our immediate observation. In passing over to
the borders of the lake, we saw near the centre
of it a large raft, and a number of canoes filled
with people. On first landing, we were surprised
not to see any women or children, the mystery of
which was now explained, as well as the singular
visit we received on first approaching this part of
the island. The person in the canoe had been
sent off as a spy, to reconnoitre us, and from the
report he made, it was thought expedient to remove the women and children, where we now saw
them at a place of safety. They did not appear
to be more than thirty in number, and the men on
the island did not exceed fifteen. The men re-

sembled the inhabitants of Clarence Island, in dress, colour, and every thing, except that they had a sickly look, and, in strength and activity, seemed much their inferiors. Their canoes were also the same. Like the inhabitants of the Duke of Clarence Island, they had nothing amongst them that indicated a visit of white men before. The cocoa-nut, except when they catch fish, is their only food. No bread-fruit trees were seen growing upon either island. They exchanged for iron hoop and old nails, their rude shell ornaments, mats, cocoa-nuts, and fishing nets. We witnessed several instances of dishonesty, practised by them upon us, and each other. Their fishing-nets, which were beautifully wrought, they had concealed, from the apprehension that we would plunder them; but when they had made acquaintance with us, and found that our disposition towards them was friendly, persons, to whom the nets did not belong, would purloin, and bring them to us, in exchange for pieces of iron hoop. Not long afterwards the owner would discover his net in the possession of one of our people, and claim it as his property, or demand a gratuity. In this way, they made us pay in some instances three or four times for the same thing, frequently (we began to suspect) pretending a fraud had been committed upon them, whilst they themselves were the rogues. We saw no animals or birds upon

H

the island, but presented them with a pair of pigs, male and female, with which they were very much pleased, and before we left them, so far acquired their confidence, that they came amongst us without fear, and, in many instances, became troublesome by their familiarity. The only water we saw on the island was in a few trunks of cocoanut trees, the stumps of which had been hollowed out, and from whence we supposed that, in time of drought, if not always, they are supplied with this important necessary of life. We regretted the more that we could not find a sufficient supply here, as the thinly populated state of the island would admit of sending our parties on shore, without the least apprehension of hostility from the natives, and because the landing was such, as to permit the embarkation, without great labour, or risk of losing boats.

As the Duke of York Island was not inhabited, when discovered by Commodore Byron, thirty-five years previous to the visit of the Dolphin, it is reasonable to suppose, from the strong resemblance of the natives to those of Clarence Island, their dress and canoes being the same, that they came from thence at no very distant period. The distance of these islands from each other, is only about forty miles, and a canoe, being driven from one in the direction of the other, in tempestuous weather, would soon be in sight of it. Towards evening in returning on board, we found, to our regret, that the tide had risen two or three feet over the coral bank, and it became difficult for us to see the holes, some of which, being now filled with water, were deep enough to be attended with danger. Besides this, the surf, as is usual upon these coral banks, had increased with the rising tide to such a degree, that we found it difficult to embark. Guided by our observation, in the morning, however, we got on board safely, with the exception of some trifling accidents. The most serious of which was having the boat bilged against the rocks.

At four, P. M. on the 31st of October, we got under way, and steered to thé westward. For several days the weather was squally, and the wind variable, shifting suddenly to all points of the compass, and blowing at times with great violence. We experienced strong currents setting in different directions, which were now a cause of serious alarm to us, as we should soon be surrounded by reefs and chains of islands, all low, and to be seen only for a few miles on a clear day. On the 9th of November, Byron's Island was seen, at 8 P. M. six miles from us, and soon afterwards the shore was lighted up with a number of fires. The surf was beating heavily upon the weather-shore. We stood off and on until morning, when, having been driven to leeward by a strong current, we beat up for the island, passing several canoes on our way, and having a great many others in different directions to windward, running down for us. At meridian, we were close in with the land, where we beat about for several hours, looking for anchorage. Once we tacked, in three fathoms, so close to the coral bank, where was beating a heavy surf, that we could almost have jumped upon it. At 6, P. M. on the tenth, we anchored in ten fathoms, within less than a cable's length of the surf, and where the water was so clear, that we could see almost every coral rock at the bottom. Besides the rocks, it presented the appearance of a splendid landscape of trees and copse-wood, ornamented with the most lively and brilliant colours, which, affected by the swelling of the ocean, were transformed into a representation of a rich and beautiful country of mountain and valley.

Whilst we were beating about, canoes were assembling near us, in great numbers, and as soon as we anchored, came along side, the people jumping on board without the least hesitation, talking and hallooing to each other so loud, as almost to deafen us with their noise. They had not been long on board, before several of them were detected in thieving, and when threatened, seemed quite regardless of our displeasure, although it was expressed in a way calculated to make them sensible of its disagreeable consequences. They were all provided with long shark's-tooth spears, and walked about the deck with a swaggering, independent air, that seemed to challenge, at least, an equality. But few brought any thing else with them but their spears, which they would not dispose of, and altogether, their number and appearance was truly formidable. At sunset, we sent them off, and they all returned to their respective islets.

The appearance of Byron's Island, differed scarcely in any respect from that of the Duke of Clarence. Its dimensions and formation were perfectly similar; and, like the latter, it was inhabited by an enterprising and warlike people, whose dress, arms, canoes, and manner of life, seemed to be identically the same. The islet abreast of us was all night illuminated with numerous fires, and the air rung incessantly with the shouts of hundreds of people.

When the day dawned, the whole ocean was whitened with the little sails of canoes that were seen coming from every direction, and some of them as far as the eye could distinguish so small an object. In an hour, not less than a hundred of them were alongside, and our deck was crowded with the natives. The officer of the watch undertook to wash off the deck, which he found altogether impracticable: not a word could be understood for the noise that they made, and when they were pushed out of the way by our people, they became insolent and resentful. We were at length, obliged to resort to some little violence to clear the decks of the unruly rabble, whose disposition to thievery and violence, became every moment more difficult to repress.

An old athletic chief, whom our captain had treated with more than ordinary attention, suddenly put his arms round him, and embraced him with such herculean strength, that he was constrained to call on the men near him for assistance; in a moment, they had a rope around the old chief's neck, and broke his grasp, and the captain having enough of Indian courtesy, was well pleased to dismiss them. They still remained near us, and as many as were allowed, came alongside. They exchanged for pieces of old iron, coarse matting, flying-fish, shell ornaments, and a few of them disposed of their spears.

One fellow, who evinced an obstinate determination to come alongside, was ordered off by the sentinel, who pointed his musket at him. As soon as the musket was pointed, he raised his spear, and stood in the attitude of throwing it until the sentinel came to a shoulder, when he again took to his paddle; the musket was again presented, and the Indian, with the same promptitude, raised his spear, until the sentinel, feeling the awkwardness of his situation, reported the circumstance to an officer. I went forward, and pointing at the native a pistol loaded with very fine shot, motioned for him to retire; upon which, he raised his spear at me, and I discharged the pistol at his legs, when he dropped his arms and fled with the greatest precipitation; I afterwards remarked him outside of all the rest of the canoes, apparently afraid to come nearer the vessel. After this example, none of them seemed disposed to question the authority of a sentinel.

The islands we had seen, since our departure from the Marquesas, resembling each other so much, and none of them affording indications of water sufficient for our purposes, we began to think seriously, that we might experience great inconvenience, and perhaps suffering, before we could procure a supply; we determined, therefore, to let no opportunity escape us, of examining every island that came in our way, if it could be done without too much risk. With a view to this object, the captain pulled in shore, followed by nearly all the canoes; but when he arrived at the edge of the surf, which was so heavy as to make the landing difficult, he remarked that the people on shore, of whom a great many were assembled, had all armed themselves with spears and stones. This hostile appearance, together with the violence of the surf, made him hesitate about proceeding further, although the natives, on shore as well as those in canoes, pressed him to land. When, finally, he relinquished his object, and was about to return on board, the people on shore dashed into the water and swam off, and uniting with those in the canoes, made a violent attempt to drag the boat into the surf. The men promptly repelled them, when they dived to the bottom, and coming up, showered a volley of stones into the boat, which wounded a few of the crew slightly, and broke several pieces of the gunwale. In the midst of the excitement and confusion that prevailed, a native seized a pistol, which he struggled violently to carry off, until a musket was fired, and he was taken into the nearest canoe severely wounded; it had the effect to disperse the natives, who fled from the boat in every direction, as she returned to the schooner. When she was hoisted in, they came alongside, and some of them got on board. We commenced getting underway, and one of the anchors was already up; the other having hooked to a coral rock, the captain directed the sentinel forward, to give the musket to him, and repair to his station. A native, who had been talking to the captain, embracing a favourable opportunity, seized the musket, upon which was a fixed bayonet, and jumping overboard with it, swam towards the shore, keeping half the time under water. Muskets were fired at him, but he bore his booty safely through the surf to the coral bank, where, although he was still within striking distance, he marched away with the most perfect composure, until he disappeared in the bushes.

After this bold theft, several boats were prepared to land in search of water, and, if possible, recover the stolen property. The captain took the lead, and landed on the coral bank, with his arms and ammunition wet and useless, whilst the boat, in returning through the surf, was thrown upon the rocks, bilged, and before she finally got off, almost every timber in her broke. This fatality having attended his landing, he forbade the other boats to attempt it, choosing rather to remain in his defenceless situation, surrounded by hostile natives, to the more serious consequence of losing the remainder of his boats.

By signals concerted previous to his departure from the vessel, he directed a fire at intervals from our cannon, in the direction of a large hut that we supposed belonged to the chief. A small group of natives approached him, one of whom, a man advanced in years, came up with a green branch in his hand ; the captain demanded of him by signs the return of the musket, in reply to which, he addressed some one near him, who ran off, and in about an hour, brought it without either lock or bayonet ; these were also required, and our demand repeated occasionally by a discharge of cannon in the direction of the chief's hut. It was not long before the lock was brought, but no threats could compel them to relinquish the bayonet. The situation of the captain and his party was becoming more and more critical with every moment's delay. They were on a bank of coral a hundred yards wide, and small parties of natives, of whom great numbers were assembled in the bushes, would frequently sally out and throw stones at them. They had no other means of protection or defence than what was afforded by our guns, which were fired whenever the hostile parties made their appearance. The hustle of our shot over their heads, and the fall of cocoanut trees, proved to them the superiority of our arms over theirs, and in a measure, had the desired effect of keeping them back. One circumstance, however, convinced us that they were not yet fully sensible of this superiority, or if so, that they were intrepid to a degree that might well alarm us for the safety of our people.

When one of their parties had sallied out, there were two men walking along the beach, carrying a canoe ; a shot that was fired to drive the sallying party back, struck so near these men, that it threw the sand and gravel all over them. They laid the canoe down and looked round them for a few moments, when they took it up again and walked along, as they would have done under the most ordinary circumstances.

When the captain became impatient of his confined situation on the beach, besieged and harrassed as he constantly was by the natives, he made bold to risk an excursion back upon the island, to show the natives his disregard for them, and, at the same time, satisfy himself as to the existence of water. They did not any where oppose him or appear in numbers; a few persons were seen behind the trees, or stealing along through the thickets without any demonstration of hostility. His discoveries were few and unimportant; the only place where he found water, was in an old well, where it was stagnant and unfit for use. In the huts that he entered, were stores of dry cocoa-nuts, and a preparation of dried fish and sea-moss.

We were filled with solicitude for our party when beyond the reach of our assistance, knowing that they had no other means of safety than the opinion which might exist among the natives of their invincibility, and we were highly gratified, after an hour's watching, to see them returning to their old place of blockade—the coral bank.

It was now sundown, and the surf had increased so much that we did not believe it possible for a boat to reach the shore and return in safety; and to send men there without a prospect of their being enabled to return, would be but a useless sacrifice of lives; but here was our people on shore; the natives had followed them on their return to the beach; and their remaining after dark would probably be attended with the most serious consequences. Two men, who were good swimmers, came forward and volunteered their services to take on shore a light boat that we had, and although I might have felt unwilling to exercise authority in the performance of so hazardous a service, I was happy to accept the generous offer. They landed in safety, and the boat being deeply laden with the captain and his party, they clung with one hand to her quarter, swimming with the other, until after a severe and most doubtful struggle, she emerged from the surf, almost filled with water, and was soon afterwards alongside. It was thought that if there had been one more breaker to pass, all would have perished.

The men of Byron's Island are stout, active, and well made. They were all naked, and covered with scars. Some of them wore skull-caps, of grass, and wreaths of dry cocoa-nuts. Their ornaments were rude, and worn by but very few. They consisted of shells and beads, made of something that resembled whalebone, worn in long strings,—by some round the waist, and by others round the neck. Their hair was long and matted, and their complexion very dark. Their beard

was thin, and curled upon the chin, like that of
the negroes. A few women came round us in
canoes, who looked coarse, and almost as robust
as the men. They wore round their loins a small
mat about a foot wide, with a fringe at the bottom. But few of the men were tattooed, and they
very slightly. Their canoes were ingeniously
wrought, of a great many pieces of light wood,
which were laced together by twine, made from
the husk of the cocoa-nut; but they were so leaky
as to keep one man baling constantly. They
were very narrow, sharp at both ends, and had a
small platform of light wood, on one side, to keep
them upright. They resembled the canoes of the
Duke of York and Clarence islands, but were rather narrower, and made with better workmanship. The canoe sails, of all these islands, are
mats of straw or grass.

As soon as the captain returned on board, we
got underway, and bade adieu to Byron's Island,
and its inhabitants, whose acquaintance had been
productive of nothing but anxiety and perplexity.
We run off W. by S., and in three or four hours
made Drummond's Island, ahead, distant three or
four leagues.

At daylight, we passed a reef of considerable
extent upon the N. E. end of the island, and ran
down upon the west side of it. When we had
approached the shore, within the distance of a

league, canoes made their appearance in every direction, sailing off to us. We stood in, and found anchorage within two cables' length of the bank of coral, that stretched one or two miles from the shore, and which, at low water, was almost every where dry. Here we hove to, having in sight, along the shore, twenty or thirty large villages, besides other habitations, that were thickly interspersed amongst the trees beyond it. The island, indeed, was swarming with inhabitants, and, from its extent and forest of cocoa-nut trees, seemed well adapted to sustain a large population. It was low, and being quite level, promised but a poor prospect of affording a supply of water. We had not been long hove to, before we were surrounded by from one to two hundred canoes, having in each of them, with few exceptions, two men and a woman, the latter of whom was kept constantly employed baling the water out. They betrayed a greater degree of timidity than the natives of any island we had seen before, keeping in their canoes, at a distance from us, or approaching, with caution and distrust. At length some of them got on board, and others hung upon the sides of the vessel, talking and exchanging their cocoa-nuts, and flying-fish, for old nails, or pieces of tin. One of them, an interesting looking youth, was noticed by one of the seamen, who made him several presents, and in other respects, treated him very kindly. The youth appeared to be sensible of the favour shown him, and expressed his gratitude by smiles, and by repeatedly patting the sailor on the shoulder ; but, after this dumb show had been going on for some time, and when his patron's face was turned from him, he snatched his hat from his head, and jumped overboard with it, making his way as expeditiously as possible to the nearest canoe. The canoe took him in, and pulled off dead to windward of us, until they were out of our reach, although we threw several shot over their heads, to convince them of the danger they encountered in such bold adventures. From our first stopping place, we ran down a few miles, followed by all the canoes, which were joined by many more. Some of the natives again came on board, and one man, to whom the captain had made presents, seized upon a fixture of the waist-boat, and abruptly took his leave. He was as suddenly saluted with a charge of bird-shot, from a pistol, but manfully clung to his prize, and bore it off in triumph to his canoe. Aided by his companion, he was playing us the same trick, as the fellow who stole the sailor's hat. But a few shot over their heads brought them to, when they lay down in the bottom of the canoe, until we lowered a boat, and sent it to them. When they saw the boat approaching, they took to their paddles, and made an effort to escape; but, finding that impossible, jumped overboard, and continued diving from one side of the canoe to the other, until they were taken. They trembled excessively, expressing a great deal of alarm, upon being brought on board, and made several attempts to escape. The captain inflicted upon the thief, a punishment, that he thought might be a useful admonition to the natives, in their future intercourse with white men, when, with his companion, he jumped overboard, apparently delighted, in having escaped so well. The number and enterprising character of the people, changed our purpose of attempting to obtain a supply of water, by digging wells. And, besides the above objection, it was to be expected that, in the performance of our duty, at the Mulgrave Islands, it would be necessary for us to explore the whole group, where, within so great a compass, our wants could scarcely fail to be supplied. Accordingly, in the evening, we made sail, and, after clearing the island, hauled up to the northward and westward. The inhabitants of Drummond's and Byron's Islands, were, in all respects, similar to each other, even to their canoes and sails, the latter of which was a coarse matting of grass.

During our passage from Drummond's Island to the Mulgraves, which was of nine days' duration we had squally weather, and were constantly affected by violent currents, for which, as they were irregular, no allowance could be made. On the second day after our departure from Drummond's Island, our safety was considerably endangered from this cause. Being near a chain of small islands belonging to the Kingsmill Group, the weather thick and squally, we stretched off, calculating that, at meridian, on the following day, we should be thirty miles to the northward of them; but, to our surprise, when at meridian the weather cleared, and we got our observations, instead of being thirty miles to the northward, we were as much to the south, having been carried through them by a current at night. We were two or three days in the vicinity of the Mulgraves', laying to at night, and drifting with the current nearly as much as we advanced through the day, with light and baffling winds.

On the evening of November, the nineteenth, the welcome hail of "Land! ho!" was given, and shortly aftewards it was seen from the deck, two leagues off. It proved to be the easternmost of the Mulgraves', for which we run down on the following morning, and anchored on the lee shore, within less than a cable's length of the surf, in six fathoms water.

The island was low, of coral formation, and, in all respects, resembled Caroline, Clarence, York, Byron's, and Drummond's Islands. The inhabit-

I

ants were not numerous, and differed from all we
had seen before in dress and manners. They
gave us a most kind and hospitable reception,
freely offered whatever any of us expressed a wish
for, and in all respects acquitted themselves in a
manner highly satisfactory. Near our landing
place we had the satisfaction to find two or three
old wells of water, which, after being cleared out,
would afford us a supply without much labour in
getting it off, the landing being tolerably good.

On the twenty-first and twenty-second of November, we filled our water-casks, and, with several parties, explored the island. In our search
we found a whaler's lance, and several pieces of
old canvass ; but all our efforts to obtain a know-
ledge, from whence they came, or of the persons
who brought them, were unavailing. Some of the
natives came on board, all of whom were neatly
ornamented. They wore wreaths of flowers round
their heads, bracelets and necklaces of beautiful
shells ; a large roll of leaves, from one to two
inches in diameter, through slits in their ears, and
as a covering for their loins, two bunches of a
kind of grass, that resembled hemp, hanging below
their knees, one bunch being behind, and the
other before. Nothing was stolen by them. They
behaved in a most orderly manner, looking round
the deck inquiringly, or seated themselves, and
chatted familiarly with our people, taking pains to

make themselves understood. In their look and action they appeared to be lively and intelligent; but whenever the subject of our visit was pressed upon them, by pointing to the whaler's lance, they became silent, pretending to be ignorant of our meaning. The activity of our exploring parties, in traversing all parts of the island, and our close examination of every thing amongst them, that had belonged to the whites, produced a sensible alarm by the third day; and, besides the desertion of their habitations by some of them, a large canoe was missing, that had departed from the island during the night.

Beyond us, to the south and west, was a range of islets, as far as we could see from the mast-head, and having thoroughly explored the island, where we were anchored, completed our watering, and made such repairs upon the vessel as were necessary, we determined to proceed further in that direction. At our anchorage here the wind several times changed from blowing off shore, which, as we had not room to ride in shore of our anchor, made it, upon such occasions, necessary to get underway, and stand off. At such times, we remarked, with particular satisfaction, the advantage we possessed in our vessel, being schooner rigged, as none but a fore and after could, with the same facility, have performed the delicate operation of getting underway, and crawling off, when riding upon a lee shore, within a few fathoms of the rocks, to have touched which would inevitably have been attended with shipwreck.

Upon the island, besides cocoa-nut, there were a few bread-fruit trees, growing in great luxuriance. The golden yellow fruit, with which the females of Nooaheeva ornamented their necks, grew here in the greatest abundance, and was eaten by the natives almost constantly, who called it *bup*. A species of small rat, with a tuft of hair upon the tail, was very numerous, and so tame, that hundreds of them were constantly feeding about the huts.

The first land we approached in proceeding to the southward and westward, was a narrow islet, made up of dry reefs, and verdant spots, from one to two miles long, and two hundred yards wide. On most of the islets grew cocoa-nut, and bread-fruit trees,—the invariable indication of inhabitants. They were, however, but thinly inhabited. Some of the reefs that connected them were covered with water sufficiently for the passage of a boat. The captain landed upon the eastern extremity, where he found a few people, most of whom fled at his approach, and such as remained, were so timid, that we could hardly look upon them as the countrymen and near neighbours of the natives, who had treated us with so much kindness at our anchorage.

A small canoe came off, paddled by one man, who ventured on board, and looked round for a few minutes, when he departed, without seeming to have had any other object in view than to gratify his curiosity. We should have suspected him of being a spy, had we not believed these people too simple, to adopt such an expedient of civilization. This we, however, afterwards ascertained was the capacity in which he came, having been sent by the principal chief of all the Mulgrave Group.

The schooner coasted along the islands, keeping way with the captain, who continued on to the westward, examining all parts of it. Beyond, in what we afterwards ascertained was an inland sea of great extent; several large sail canoes were discovered coming from a distant islet. The captain crossed the reef into the inland sea, where he found the water smooth, but every where filled with shoals of coral. Without indicating a wish to examine the canoes, which might have caused them to put back, he soon afterwards returned on board, and another boat was sent to continue the examination of the islet, as we advanced. The officer prevailed upon some natives, that he met with, to come near him, and one of them gave him, in return for a present, some glass beads. Upon arriving at the western extremity of the islet, the captain put off for the shore, where

he found four large canoes hauled up on the beach,
and those he had seen before, coming over the
inland sea, just in the act of landing. As we
afterwards ascertained, it was the high chief of
the Mulgrave Group, with from fifty to a hundred
of his chiefs and warriors, on a cruise of observation, to satisfy himself who, and what we were,
and what was the object of our visit to his lonely
and unfrequented isle. None of the chiefs had
any thing to distinguish them, so that we knew
not but that they were here upon some ordinary
pursuit, otherwise, their presence would have excited in us a much more lively interest. As it
was, we were gratified to have an opportunity of
seeing so many of the natives, with their canoes,
which we could examine, for proofs of the crew of
the Globe having landed upon these islands, of
which we were already pretty well satisfied from
what we had seen. The fact was satisfactorily
proved in a few minutes afterwards, by our discovering upon the platform of their canoes the
lids of several sailors' chests. On a further examination, pieces of cloth and ash-spars were also
found. The natives were watching our every
look and motion, and notwithstanding their pretended apathy and indifference, could not conceal
the intense excitement that our close examination
produced amongst them, It soon gave rise to an
animated conversation, which was accompanied

with angry looks, and the only satisfaction they gave us, when we pointed to the chest-lids, was a vacant stare, or a few words of their island language not more intelligible. Not far from the beach was a pleasant grove of cocoa-nut and bread-fruit trees, through which was scattered a number of neat little Indian huts. One of them, near the shore, was frequented by a great many of the natives, with whom our people freely mingled. It was about ten feet high, and above the ground; had a small garret, which was screened from observation by a floor of sticks, thickly interwoven with leaves. Although most of the huts had been examined by our men, it was our good or ill fortune, that this, where so many were constantly assembled, should escape observation. We should there have found one of the men, as he afterwards informed us, for whom we were so anxiously looking; but the discovery might have been attended with bloodshed, and, perhaps, fatal consequences to our shore party, than whom the natives were much more numerous.

William Lay, one of the Globe's crew, had been brought to this islet, by the chiefs, to be used as circumstances might suggest. He was concealed in the garret of the hut, and guarded by a number of old women, who were directed, the first whisper of noise that he made, to put him to death, the chiefs having also denounced their heaviest vengeance upon him, if he should, in any way, disclose the secret of his being there. He lay in this unhappy situation for several hours, listening to the interchange of opinion amongst his countrymen, from whose conversation he was informed of the character of our vessel, and the object of her cruise.

Towards sun-down, when our parties were weary with the labour of the day, they repaired on board for the night, and the natives, getting into their canoes, took their departure from the islet, and steered away, over the inland sea, until they were lost in the horizon. We stood off and on during the night, and, at nine in the morning, anchored in nine fathoms water, near our place of landing. Here there was a channel into the inland sea, having nearly water enough for the schooner, and through which we made an unsuccessful attempt to pass. Our situation was now becoming very unpleasant. It was necessary for us to have parties on shore, exploring the islands, and the remainder of the crew was quite insufficient to get the vessel underway,—an expedient indispensable, whenever the wind came on shore, as the anchorage hardly ever extended more than half a cable's length from it. That we might lose nothing from delay or want of perseverance, however, soon after we came to, an officer, with a party of eleven men, attended by a boat to take

them over the drowned reefs, was sent to march
round, and explore the islets, that formed a continued chain to the southward and westward of
us. We felt a conviction, from the conduct of
the natives, that they were unwilling to give us
the intelligence we required, and that we must
depend entirely upon our industry and good fortune, for any discovery we might make. In the
evening we sent a boat to communicate with our
party, but they had advanced so far, that she returned without seeing any of them.

On the following day, November the twenty-
fifth, the weather clear and pleasant, a boat was
sent with refreshments to our exploring party, who
were overtaken at the distance of ten miles from
us, just commencing their morning's march. The
islets, thus far, were narrow, not averaging a
quarter of a mile in breadth, and but thinly inhabited. Our party were pleased with the conduct
of the natives they had seen. They gave them
cocoa-nuts, without receiving any thing in return,
and in the evening, when they stopped to repose
for the night, provided them with huts to sleep in.
The officer of the party, in the course of the day's
march, found a mitten, with the name of Rowland
Coffin marked on it, who, by referring to a list
of the Globe's crew, proved to be one of the boys
left with the mutineers. From the place where
the party was found, the extent of the island could

not be seen. I landed at the settlement where we were anchored, and found the huts nearly all deserted. Such of the natives, as remained, seemed disposed to be very friendly, and followed me to the beach, where I shot a few sand-snipe, which drew from them loud shouts of applause, on witnessing the effect of my musket. Near the huts I observed a number of small white cranes, one of which I shot, supposing them to be wild, but afterwards regretted it very much, on learning that they were domesticated, and held in great reverence by the natives.

At five in the morning, November the twenty-sixth, a squall arose from the eastward, which struck the vessel adrift, in the direction of the trending of the land, and, dragging off the bank, we hove the anchor up, and stood along shore to the westward. When we had run fifteen or twenty miles, we came up with our party, to whom we sent refreshments, and proceeded on, passing several remarkable points.

At three, P. M., we came to, under a point, by which we were somewhat protected from the sea, in ten fathoms of water, and about thirty fathoms from the coral rocks, where there was but three feet. We were considerably in advance of our party, whom we had now determined should march round the whole circle of islets, if information of the mutineers should not sooner be ob-

tained.   In front of us the islet was wider than
any we had seen elsewhere, and presented a no-
ble forest of cocoa-nut, interspersed every where
with the broad green leaves of the bread-fruit
tree, which indicated a most luxuriant growth.
Huts were scattered about through the trees, and
some close to the shore, forming a peaceful and
romantic scene.   The landing was good at low
water, and practicable at high tide.   As far as
we could see to the westward, the land still continued.

The surgeon, who was very much debilitated,
when we sailed from the coast of Peru, had gradually, and almost imperceptibly, become more
feeble, and for some time past believed that he
had a disease of the liver.   Until within two days
of coming to our present anchorage, he discharged
his ordinary duties, in attending the sick, when his
mind began to fail, and it was evident to us that the
period of his existence was near its close.   He lay
for a time in a state of insensibility, receiving the
little aid that his friends could afford him ; and at
forty-five minutes after four, P. M., November
the twenty-seventh, breathed his last, deeply
lamented by all the crew, to whom he had greatly
endeared himself, by kind and assiduous atten-
tions, even when he was extremely ill, and knew
that he was fast hastening to the close of life.
In the morning, I took a party of men on shore,

and in a grove, at the foot of a wide-spreading bread-fruit tree, made the narrow bed of our departed messmate. At nine, the vessel struck adrift, and dragged off the bank. When she again stood in towards the shore, we landed, with as many of the officers and men as could be spared to bury the doctor's remains, with the honours of war. The natives assembled, to the number of twenty or thirty, and followed us to the grave, watching all our motions with an expression of great surprise. They were silent until the first discharge of musketry, when they burst into loud shouts and laughter, for which we drove them back, with threats of punishment, a considerable distance from us, where they afterwards remained quiet. At the foot and head of the grave we planted seeds of orange, lemon, and cheramoya, and upon the bread-fruit tree, at the head of it, carved his name, rank, and the vessel to which he belonged. Below this we spiked, firmly upon the tree, a brass plate, with his name, age, the vessel to which he belonged, and the day of his death inscribed upon it. A little to the eastward of the grave we had the satisfaction to find two springs of excellent water.

On the following morning our party arrived, and, after receiving refreshment, continued on to the northward and westward. They crossed a long reef, that connected the islet abreast of us

with another, at the distance of a few miles, that
had the appearance of a large settlement, from
the immense cocoa-nut forests that rose in that
direction.   Soon after crossing the reef, and arriving at the extreme east end of the islet, where
it was narrow and sandy, they suddenly came to
a place that was strewed with several hundreds of
staves of beef and pork barrels, and old pieces of
canvass and cloth.   In advancing a little further,
they found a skeleton, lightly covered with sand,
and a box, containing a few Spanish dollars. The
natives, some of whom had been constantly following our party, and occasionally mingling with
them, and administering, as well as they could to
their wants, upon approaching this place disappeared, or were seen at a distance, skulking
through the bushes.   These discoveries excited
the liveliest expectation of soon making others
more satisfactory, and proceeding a mile further,
they found an unoccupied hut, where, night approaching, they encamped.   Early in the morning they took up their line of march, and had not
gone far, when it was evident that the natives
were preparing for hostilities.   Groups of them
were frequently seen at a distance, armed with
spears and stones, and holding animated discus-
sions.   They were much more numerous than
our party, who, upon examining their ammunition,
found it was wet, and that the few arms they had,

which were no other than a pistol, for each man,
were also wet, and unfit for immediate use. The
officer, therefore, determined to retreat to the
place of his night's encampment, until he could
despatch information of his situation, and ask for
a reinforcement and ammunition. On arriving
where he had spent the night, he found that the
hut he had occupied was gone, and also that a
large sail canoe, he left there, had been taken
away. Not a single person was any where to be
seen. Here he remained, sending two of his party
to the schooner, which was now several miles
from him. A little after meridian, we received
them on board, and heard, with great interest,
the information they gave. There was no doubt
in our minds, that this was the place where the
mutineers, and others of the Globe's crew, had
been left,—but where are they now?—was a
question, which naturally occurred to us. We
had given the natives no cause, to excite them to
hostility; but, on the contrary, had taken every
means that suggested itself, to gain their confidence and esteem. If they wished to make war
upon us, opportunities had been frequently presented, when our exploring party might have been
assailed by overpowering numbers, with a prospect of success, of which they had not availed
themselves, and here they were now apparently
wavering between peace and war, just at the mo-

ment of our discovering the place where our countrymen had been. We knew not how to account for
this change in their conduct, but by supposing that
the mutineers were amongst them, and that, from
our near approach, they were becoming alarmed
for their safety, and had roused the natives to
war, with the hope of defending themselves by
open combat. If this supposition were true, and
it seemed very probable, the situation of our party
was very critical, and no time was to be lost in
giving them the aid they asked for, and renewing
our search with redoubled activity. The launch
was hoisted out, and fitted with all possible expe-
dition, and at four, P. M., November twenty-
ninth, sailed with two officers and eleven men,
together with the three belonging to the party,
being all that we were willing to spare from the
schooner, as a bold attempt upon her by a large
party of the natives, led on by an enterprising
and desperate chief, might have placed her and
the lives of all her crew in the greatest jeopardy.
I crossed the reef, which was sufficiently over-
flown by the high tide, to admit of it, and ran
down in the inland sea to the encampment of our
party, where I arrived at eight in the evening, and
found them all safe ; but looking for our appearance, with the greatest anxiety. I allowed the
boat's crew to land, and get their supper in company with those on shore, preparatory to com-

mencing their night's work. When we were prepared for our departure, and had embarked, I was
greatly chagrined on examining the boat, to find
that the shore party, to whom I had brought fresh
arms and ammunition, had, in their over-anxiety
to be well supplied, deprived me of part of mine,
and I was under the necessity of landing, and
searching, not only the men, but even the bushes,
before I found them.

Our party had acquired no information since
morning, but from the discoveries that had already
been made, we felt satisfied, that on the following
day, we should find other traces of the mutineers.
In taking my departure, I stretched off with a fine
breeze, but it was blowing directly from the point
to which I wished to steer. I suffered the men to
lay down and refresh themselves with sleep,
whilst midshipman S. and myself steered the boat,
and to my regret, in returning back towards the
shore from whence I had started, discovered that
we had lost ground; besides, our boat being
clumsy and badly fitted, we found that we had to
contend with a strong current. I got the oars
out, therefore, and pulled dead to windward until
day-light, when having proceeded about six miles,
we again made sail to the northward and eastward,
close haul upon a wind; it gradually veered, until I could head for an island eight or ten miles
from us, which just appeared above the horizon.

and where I designed to land and give the men breakfast. When within two or three miles of the island, I observed a number of canoes leaving places nearer to me and landing upon it. Two canoes had put off from thence, and were standing for me as I was beating with my clumsy boat to weather an intervening coral reef; they were manned with about twenty natives, all armed with spears and stones. When they had approached me pretty near, and were passing under my lee, I ran alongside to examine them, for which they gave us a great many cross looks. As soon as I suffered them to depart, they immediately returned to the shore from whence they came, and where I not long afterwards discovered about twenty canoes that would carry from twenty to forty men each.

The canoes I had boarded, sailed at least three miles to my one, and I now discovered the impossibility of possessing ourselves of the mutineers of the Globe, whilst they, or the natives, if friendly to them, had the disposal of such fleet vessels, with which to avoid us whenever our too near approach endangered their safety. I determined, therefore, to take possession of all that were now assembled, even though I should be opposed by the natives, and reduced to the necessity of measuring our strength with them.

The island was small, producing but few cocoa-

K

nut trees, and having but a small number of huts
upon it, notwithstanding which, there were several
hundreds of people assembled ;—a great crowd,
considering the thinly populated state of the islands.
But as this large assemblage could only have been
brought together from some extraordinary cause,
I determined to land and search their huts, and
look round, before I made so wide a breach with
them, as must necessarily result from the seizure
of their canoes.   I was sorry to see, on our coming near them, that they were sending their women and children towards the huts, which were at
a short distance from the assemblage of natives ;
a movement that indicated a want of confidence
in us on their part, or what was still less agreeable to us, a disposition to hostility.

There was some surf on the shore where we
were about to land near the canoes, and that the
boat might be the more readily at our disposal
when we should have occasion for her after landing, I dropped an anchor, and was in the act of
veering to through the surf, when, to my astonishment, a person dressed and looking like a native, addressed us in our own language.   He was
standing upon the beach thirty or forty yards distant, and half way between us and the natives, all
of whom had seated themselves.   The first words
that we understood, were, " The Indians are going to kill you: don't come on shore unless you

are prepared to fight." The scene now presented to us, inspired an indescribable sensation; for, although we were convinced that this was one of the men we were so anxiously looking for, his sudden and unexpected appearance, his wild attire, and above all, his warning, seemed like an illusion of fancy. His hair was long, combed up, and tied in a knot on the top of his head; round his loins, he wore a large mat, finely wrought, and the use of cocoa-nut oil, and the action of a tropical sun, for nearly two years, had made his skin almost as dark as that of the natives. He earnestly repeated, several times, that we must not land unless we were prepared to fight, and described the plan the natives had concerted with him, which was, to prevail upon us to come on shore and seat ourselves amongst them, when, at a given signal, they would all rise and knock us on the head with stones. This statement was probable enough, but the suspicion that this was one of the mutineers, very naturally occurred to our minds, with the questions, " Why have we not found him before? and, why does he not now fly to us for protection, if he is innocent?"—forgetting that our contemptible numbers precluded all idea of safety to him, if opposed by the numerous assemblage of natives by whom he was surrounded. I asked his name, which he told me was William Lay, and that he was one of the crew of the Globe. His stature and juvenile appearance, answered the description we had of him. I told him to come to the boat, but he said that he was afraid of the natives, who had directed him not to advance any nearer to us. I then directed him to run to us and we would protect him ; but he declined, saying, that the natives would kill him with stones before he could get there. During all this time, they thought he was arranging their plan for us to come on shore, and called out frequently to him to know what we said ; to which, he replied in a way calculated to suit his purpose.

After discharging and re-loading our pistols, with one of which and a cartridge-box each man was provided, we landed, and marched up to the place where Lay was standing. Still doubting whether he were not more foe than friend, and determined that, under any circumstances, he should not escape, I received him with my left hand, presenting, at the same time, a cocked pistol to his breast. I was not insensible to the sentiment my harsh reception was calculated to inspire ; but circumstanced as I was, I could not risk every thing in preference to inflicting a momentary pang, keenly as it might be felt. I repeated the question, " Who are you?" to which he replied, "I am your man," and burst into tears. I told him then to say to the natives, that if they rose from their seats, or threw a stone, we would shoot them all; but the poor fellow, delirious with joy for the moment, knew not what he said, and, instead of obeying my command, called out in half English, and half Island language, in broken sentences, most of which was unintelligible to us; amongst other things, he exclaimed, "they are going to kill me, they are going to kill me." I ordered him to be silent, and then asked, why he told them we were going to kill him.— Recollecting himself immediately, he begged my pardon, declaring that he knew not what he was saying. By this time, some of the natives had risen, and were becoming very animated and violent in their conversation and gestures. Two or three of them advanced towards us; I pointed my pistol at them, and made Lay repeat my threat. which had the desired effect on all but one old man, who, unarmed, advanced in defiance of me. Lay desired me to suffer him to approach, which he did, and taking hold of Lay's hand with both of his, he asked what his countrymen were going to do with him. Lay explained to him, in a few words, as clearly as he could, at which the old man seemed much affected. This was his benefactor, the person to whom he was indebted for life; and the poor fellow seemed not wanting in sensibility or gratitude, at the moment of their parting. He embraced him affectionately, told him that he would see him again before he departed, and wept like a child. I was unwilling to remain longer than was absolutely necessary, lest the natives, when they had recovered from their first surprise, should conceive a contempt for our small number, and make trial of our strength, in which I knew they would be much superior to us, if they were determined and brave, as the first discharge of our pistols would place us upon an equality with the same number as ourselves. I therefore cut short Lay's interview with his friend, and hastened him to the boat; there he wept for joy, and gave us several proofs of the agitated state of his mind. His first impulse, which did great credit to his heart, was, to inquire if his friends were well, and then recollecting that it was probable none of us knew them, told us he belonged to East Saybrook, Connecticut, and asked if any of us were acquainted in that section of the country. He several times repeated the same questions, forgetful that he had asked them before, and that we had replied in the negative. When his mind was a little composed, we made inquiries of him respecting the rest of the Globe's crew, who had been left on the island; to which he answered, that they were all dead except Cyrus H. Huzzy, who was on an island a few miles to windward of us, and now full in sight. He asked, with an expression of great solicitude, if we would go for Huzzy, and when I told him we would, it seemed to afford him not less pleasure than his own deliverance. He stated that he and Huzzy both knew that we were in search of them, and that our vessel was a man of war. He said that the chiefs had sent spies on board of the schooner every day when it was practicable, who had communicated to them the number of guns we carried, and, within a very few, the number of which the crew consisted. They had apprised them of the force and conduct of our exploring party, descending to the minutest particulars, and even describing most of the individuals on board. They had seriously debated the question of making war upon us several times, and always consulted Lay and Huzzy as to the propriety of it, and what would probably be their prospect of success. They dissuaded them from it, of course, and filled them with apprehension, by declaring, repeatedly, that we were invincible, and that there was scarcely any thing we could not accomplish with our six-pounders; they even made them believe, trifling as our armament was, that we could sink the islands with our cannon: so ready is the human mind to receive for truth what it cannot comprehend, if recommended by superior intelligence, though it may be at variance with every thing in nature or reason.

The natives were told to let us go where we

pleased, without molesting us in any way, to give us whatever we asked for, and, at all times, to show themselves friendly to us.   They had strictly pursued the course of conduct pointed out to them by the young white men, in whose superior know-ledge of us and our prowess, they placed every reliance ; but still they doubted the probability of conciliating our friendship in the sequel, and adhered tenaciously to the idea of accomplishing our destruction in some way, to make their own security the more certain.   With this object, a variety of plans were submitted at different times, to Lay and Huzzy, by those amongst the chiefs esteemed the wisest and bravest, all of which were discouraged, and the success of such an under-taking in any way, as frequently declared to be utterly hopeless.

One of their plans was, to get alongside of us at night, unobserved, and with some of the sharp instruments they had obtained from the Globe, make a hole in the bottom of the vessel, and sink her ; when, they very truly believed, that those who were not drowned, would be an easy prey to them, and that the party on shore, unaided by the schooner, might soon be overcome and destroyed by their superior numbers.

Another of their plans, and the most plausible one, was, to assemble secretly all the canoes of the islands, at some point not distant from us, and approaching under cover of the night, surprise and board us.

If this last plan had been put into execution, in a dark night, it is possible that it might have succeeded, as we could hardly have seen them in time to use our cannon, and the fire of musketry which they had heard before, would probably not have driven them back when they had advanced near to us, particularly if, as might be apprehended, at night, the fire were not directed effectively. They would not have found us entirely unprepared ; for, under the impression that the mutineers were still living, and on terms of friendship with the natives, we were on the lookout for such an attempt being made, as it seemed to be the only means by which they could possibly escape, and the plan which would most naturally occur to desperate men in their situation.

In advancing towards the island where we expected to find Huzzy, Lay told us that the island where we found him was a favourite place for fishing at a particular season, when numerous shoals of fish swam upon its shore. Our schooner was anchored at the place of residence of the high chief, who, with those we found assembled upon the small island, had fled there to avoid us. The boat's crew being oppressed with fatigue and hunger, I landed upon a dry reef, after proceeding a few miles to give them rest and refreshment. It was painful to witness Lay's anxiety to depart, who, fearing a messenger might be despatched to the chief who had Huzzy in custody, kept his eyes fixed upon us with an anxious, hurrying look, and several times expressed his fears that the chiefs might have the boldness to attempt his rescue. On finishing our frugal repast, we pulled up under an uninhabited point of Lugoma's Island, (this was the name of Huzzy's chief,) which, having passed without observation, an ample bay, upon the shore of which was situated the village of the chief, opened to our view; and, to our great joy, the only sail canoe in his possession, was seen hauled up on the beach. For a few moments, no one was seen; but when we were in the act of landing, Lugoma and several old women came walking down to the beach, attracted by the strange and unexpected appearance of our boat. They were struck with the utmost consternation at beholding Lay, who was still in his native dress; and the old women began calling out, in a loud tone, demanding of him what he was doing there, and what we wanted. Before he had time to reply to them, I got out of the boat, and taking hold of Lugoma, and pointing a pistol at him, bade Lay say to him, that unless Huzzy was brought to me immediately, I would kill him. He begged that I would not hurt him, and said Huzzy was near and should come to me. The old women, alarmed for the safety of the chief, instantly ran off, calling aloud for Huzzy. It was but a few minutes before he appeared, walking towards us, with his fine yellow hair hanging in ringlets about his shoulders, and his person quite naked, with the exception of a piece of blanket, tied round his loins. When he had approached sufficiently near, and I said to him, " Well, young man, do you wish to return to your country ?" his eyes filled with tears as he replied, " Yes, sir ; I know of nothing that I have done for which I should be afraid to go home."

As soon as Lugoma felt relieved from his apparently dangerous situation, he began to express his solicitude for Huzzy, begging that I would not hurt him ; and when he was assured that no injury was intended towards his son, as he called Huzzy, entreated me not to take him away. The old women united with the chief in the expression of their wishes, and seemed, by their loud talk and significant gestures, to insist upon the white man's remaining with them. The scene was an interesting one, and we found a picturesque group assembled on a beautiful lawn, in front of a number of huts, surrounded by cocoa-nut and bread-fruit trees. Huzzy owed his life to the native chief; he had been in the condition of a slave to him for two years. To him he was indebted for many acts of kindness, some of which he had requited by his industry in his service, and some had been cancelled by harsh treatment ; yet, still he stood in a delicate situation towards the chief. The saving of his life alone, conferred an obligation upon him, which could scarcely be repaid by long and faithful services. The chief evidently appeared to regard him as his son, and when the moment of our departure arrived, and he saw we were determined to take our countryman with us, he joined tears to entreaties, saying he should weep long and bitterly for him. He told Huzzy that he must come back again, and asked me if I would bring him. As the only way in which I could get clear of so strange a petition, urged with so much feeling, I promised to bring him back if his mother consented to his return. With this, he appeared to be tolerably well satisfied, and we were about returning to the boat, when Lugoma took Huzzy aside to talk to him privately. When their interview was ended, I asked Huzzy what the chief had been saying to him ; to which he replied, that he had been reminding him how difficult it would be for him to get along with his work without him, and that he must return as soon as he could, and bring with him some axes, guns, and cloths, such as his countrymen wore. " I have promised to bring them," said he, " when I return, and he is quite satisfied." When we

were ready to depart, to conciliate the good will
of the female part of Lugoma's family, I presented
them with a variety of trifles, such as finger-rings,
glass beads, &c., for which, in return, they loaded
me with a profusion of small mats, and rude shell
ornaments, accompanied with many expressions
of thankfulness and regard. When I came to
take leave of Lugoma, I presented him with a
jack-knife. With the exception of an axe, I
could have given him nothing more valuable, and
it gained for me his unreserved confidence. He
immediately proposed going with me to the
schooner, and got into the boat with his son, a lad
eight years old. Huzzy took with him a musket
and a Bible, the only things he had saved at the
massacre. The first had been preserved for him
by the chief, who thought that with this in Huzzy's hands, although he had no powder, he was a
match for all his enemies; and the Bible he had
clung to himself, and had kept as the companion
of his lonely hours. The Bible was more an object of curiosity to the natives than any thing else
they found in the possession of the white men :
they often inquired of Huzzy what it was, its use,
&c., and his explanations seemed only to increase
their superstition and aversion to it. They were
never pleased to see him retire to the garret of
his little hut, to read it, as was his custom; and invariably remonstrated with him against it. They

urged him frequently to destroy it, and when he refused, they threatened to do it themselves. As the reason of their dislike, they said it would bring spirits round the house that would kill or hurt some of the family. Huzzy told them, that if they destroyed it, the Great Spirit would come and kill them all; to which he was probably indebted for its preservation.

I was walking, back of the huts, over a level green spot, enclosed by cocoa-nut trees, when Lugoma came to me in great haste, and with a disturbed look beckoned me to come away, at the same time saying to Huzzy, that I must not go there: it was a place for the dead; my presence would disturb them, and bring spirits round his huts; I indulged his superstition, and walked off.

Lugoma was about thirty years of age, of moderate stature, square built, with low forehead, and flat nose; having an expression of countenance that indicated intelligence and enterprize. Huzzy gave him the character of being very passionate, inveterate in his enmities, fierce and determined in his hostility, but firmly attached to his friends, and possessing a benevolent heart. He often became offended with Huzzy, in their ordinary occupation, and upon such occasions would use violent language, and sometimes threaten to kill him; but, when his passion subsided, would be very sorry for what he had said, and soothe Huzzy by telling him not to be afraid; he would not hurt him. Once, however, in working their canoe, when something went wrong, he raised a paddle and struck Huzzy with it, upon which, the poor fellow, slave as he was, gave way to his indignant feelings, and was in the act of repaying the chief's violence with interest, who, seeing that he had gone too far with the high-spirited white man, and that his life was menaced, begged him not to strike, declaring that he would never again raise his hand against him; and the quarrel was amicably settled by Huzzy's telling him, that if ever he did, he would kill him. From this story, I thought there might be some truth in the one which Huzzy told me was one day related to him by Lugoma's son, the boy that was in the boat with us. We had a mulatto lad on board of the schooner, and at the time our contemplated capture was spoken of amongst the natives, this little boy told Huzzy that his father was going to save the life of the mulatto boy, and then kill him as he was getting too large. The mulatto boy was a great favourite amongst the natives, and upon several occasions, quarrels had arisen amongst the chiefs who should have him, when in the presence of Lay or Huzzy they were debating the question of our capture.

The day was far advanced when we left Lugoma's Island, and stood along the shores of the islets to intercept the land party whom we met at no very great distance, making rapid marches. We landed to inform them of our success, and that their labour was at an end, in which they could not but rejoice with us, although they were extremely disappointed that they should not themselves have been the fortunate persons, after all the toil they had experienced in the search. We put off and made sail in both our boats, and as the canoes were all still upon the beach of the island from whence we had taken Lay, I intended to land and get his musket, which, in the hurry of our departure, he had forgotten. No sooner, however, did the natives see both our boats standing towards them, than they put off with all their canoes, and bore away directly before the wind. We made all sail in chase, but soon perceived that they were leaving us very fast; and, as night was coming on, we made the experiment of a few musket shots, fired over their heads, with the hope of bringing them to. Instead of answering the desired purpose, it served only to increase their alarm, and the weather becoming squally, we suffered them to depart without further pursuit. I had cause to regret that I had fired; for from the first discharge, poor Lugoma was in the greatest agony, for fear we were going to kill him, as well as the rest of the chiefs. All the explanations that Lay and Huzzy could make, and all their assurances of my friendship, could not quiet him. Several times he would have taken his son and jumped overboard, had we allowed him to do so. Whenever I went to the stern of the boat where he was sitting, he repeated to me again and again that he was my good friend, and that I must not kill him; my replying that I would not hurt him, that I was his friend, &c., had not the least effect; it only caused him again to repeat what he had before told me of, his being my friend, and that I must not kill him.

The numerous shoals of coral, with the violence of the wind, rendering it somewhat dangerous to run in the dark, I determined to come to for the night, as we were yet a long distance from the schooner. For this purpose, we stood in towards the place where, on the preceding night, we had met the exploring party. Lugoma no sooner found himself so near the shore, than he became more earnest than ever in his petition to be permitted to land with his son, although he was more than twenty miles from his home. I would have allowed him to leave us, had I not been apprehensive of the hostility of his countrymen; I knew not but by his aid in piloting them to our night's encampment, we might be surprised before morning, and my resolution to keep him was confirmed, when it was reported to me, by some men who had landed from the other boat, that one

L

or more natives had been seen near us, skulking through the bushes. We also determined, not to trust ourselves on shore, but to lay in the boat, and make an awning of our sails, to screen us from the heavy showers that were frequently coming over, in the best manner we could.— When we had finished our repast, we hauled off and anchored, but not to sleep. Our awning was but poorly calculated for shelter, and the showers that constantly succeeded each other, kept us too wet and cold for rest; besides this, I was frequently reminded of Lugoma's presence, who made me pay dearly for his detention. He would lay no where else than alongside of me, and during the whole night, not more than ten minutes elapsed at any one time, that he did not move his hand over my face, and when he thought my attention was sufficiently awakened, call out to me, "Hitera;" a word that signified he was my good friend, nor would he suffer me to rest a moment afterwards until I had replied to him "Hitera."

We were anchored but a short distance from the place where the chief mutineer of the Globe and his murderous companions had landed— where he had fallen by their hands, and where they, in their turn, been killed by savages. It was a spot, calculated to revive, in the minds of Lay and Huzzy, the liveliest recollection of sorrows and sufferings, that no language could describe; and as we all wished to hear an account of the mutiny, and of the events that subsequently transpired, I desired Lay to favour us with the relation. Lay's narrative was as follows:

"The first that I heard of discontent on board of the ship, was a few days previous to the mutiny. I went to the maintop-mast-head, where I found Comstock; after a few moment's conversation, he said to me, 'What shall we do, William? we have bad usage: shall we take the ship, or run away?' To this I did not make much of any answer. I do not now remember what I said; I was quite inexperienced, it being my first voyage. In the afternoon, or the next morning, I heard him talking to some of the men on the forecastle about running away with him when we arrived at Fanning's Island, for which, I believe, we were then steering. This, I suppose, was for the purpose of sounding them, to find out their disposition, and who would join him in the mutiny.— From what we heard, we began to think that all was not right, and tried to get the news aft, but unfortunately did not succeed. In the afternoon, before the night on which the mutiny took place, we were on the main yard furling the mainsail, and I tried then to tell the second mate, but Paine or Comstock was between us, and I was afraid to say any thing. Comstock had, some days previous, taken his cutlass from the cabin into the forecastle; he was a boat-steerer, and used to eat in the cabin with the officers. I knew nothing more about it until twelve or one o'clock on the night that the mutiny took place; I was sleeping in the forecastle, when Rowland Coffin came and awoke me, saying I must come upon deck, they had taken the ship. I got up and went aft, where all the crew were mustered on the quarter-deck. When Comstock had told us what he had done, and what his regulations were, he said, that such as would not swear to stick by him, must go on the other side of the deck. I did not know how many were engaged in the mutiny, and believing that we should be killed if we did not swear, we all swore to stick by Comstock and obey his orders. He then told us to haul the third mate up out of the cabin; I was one that had to take hold of the rope made fast to him. We laid him in the gangway, and I thought he was dead; but when Comstock was throwing him overboard, he clung to the ship with his hands. Comstock told some one to bring an axe and cut his hands off, when he let go and went overboard. I saw him in the water astern, swimming after the ship for some time. We then made sail; Comstock was the only navigator on board. We first went to the Kingsmill Group, but did not like to stop there, as the natives were very numerous and thievish; besides, Comstock had shot one of them for stealing something; after which, he was afraid to stay amongst them. From Drummond's Island, of the Kingsmill Group, we came directly to the Mulgraves, and made this part of them, where we anchored and commenced landing the stores.

"The crew of the Globe consisted of between twenty-five and thirty; but the only persons engaged in the mutiny were Comstock, Paine, Oliver, and the black steward, (Lilliston, who was one of the mutineers he did not mention.) It was midnight, and previous to descending to the cabin, one of the number was placed as a sentinel at the cabin door, with an axe, Comstock saying to a young brother who was at the helm, that if he did not keep the ship in her course, he would kill him as soon as he came on deck. Comstock killed the captain by striking him on the forehead with an axe whilst he was sleeping, having first locked the mates up in their state-rooms, that they might not escape. He then went with the other mutineers, and, I believe, cut the throats of the first and second mates, and shot the third mate. I did not see any but the third mate, and was told that the others were thrown out of the cabin windows.

"Not many days after the mutiny, the black steward was detected in the cabin loading a pistol which was forbidden on pain of death; and on being asked by Comstock what he intended doing with it, he replied, at first, "Nothing;" but, when questioned more closely, he said that he had heard Smith and some one else say, they intended to take the ship. Smith and the other person named by the steward, were called up by Comstock, and asked if they had threatened to take the ship; to which they replied in the negative, insisting that they had never intimated or intended any thing of the kind. Comstock declared that such an offence could not go unpunished, and that the steward must be tried by a court martial; he thereupon told the steward to choose one man, and said that he would choose another, and that the two should sentence the steward to such punishment as the offence merited. The two men were accordingly chosen, the steward selecting Rowland Coffin for his advocate, and Comstock, Paine for his. After hearing the evidence, and deliberating for a short time, they found the steward guilty, and sentenced him to be hung at the yard-arm until he was dead. Immediately afterwards, all hands were called to witness the execution; and the steward was taken forward and given fourteen seconds to make his peace with God.* The foretop-mast steering sail haulyards were overhauled down and tied round the steward's neck, and Comstock, after making every

---

* When the steward was informed of his sentence, he asked Comstock how long a time he would give him to make his peace with God?—" Fourteen seconds !" was the reply.

body take hold of the haulyards, held the fourteen second glass in one hand, and his cutlass in the other. When the glass was out, he gave the signal for the people to run away with the haulyards, by striking the ship's bell with his cutlass, and, in a moment, the criminal was run up to the yard-arm.

"After the death of the officers, Comstock made us all live in the cabin with him, where the mutineers used to sing, and carouse, and tell over the story of the murder, and what they had dreamed. Paine and Oliver, who could scarcely ever sleep, spoke with horror of their dreams, and of ghosts that appeared to them at night; but Comstock always made light of it, and appeared to exult in what he had done. He said once, that the captain came to him with his wounded and bloody head, and showed him what he had done, when he told the captain to depart and never come again, or he would kill him a second time.

"After our arrival here, we made a raft of two whale-boats and some spars, and on the first or second day, landed thirty or forty barrels of beef and pork, sails, rigging, and a variety of other articles, when Comstock having pitched a tent on shore, commenced with the mechanics to work on a whale-boat that he was going to raise upon and make larger. Paine was displeased with his doing this so soon, and sent word to him that he had

better discharge the ship, and then work upon
the boats. This greatly enraged Comstock, who
hailed the ship for a boat, and on her being sent
to him, came on board. There he and Paine had
a violent quarrel, and Paine dared him to take a
musket and go on shore with him and fight it out,
which Comstock refused to do. When he landed,
being afraid that Paine and Oliver would kill him
if he slept in the tent, he went off to pass the
night with the natives ; in his absence, Paine and
Oliver agreed to shoot him when he came back ;
accordingly, on the following morning, he was
seen coming along the beach alone, and when he
had arrived within good gun-shot, they commenced firing at him ; without changing his pace,
he continued to advance, and drawing his cutlass,
called out to Paine to stop firing and he would
make peace with him ; Paine, however, continued
to fire, and, at the third or fourth discharge, Comstock fell lifeless upon his face, a ball having
pierced his heart. Fearing that he might not be
quite dead, and perhaps would get up again, Paine
ran up to him with an axe, and cut off the back
of his neck. He was buried close to the tent, in
the manner he had often expressed a wish to be,
with all his clothes on, and his cutlass hung to his
side. Upon first landing, he had fixed upon a
scite for a town, and amongst other public build-
ings that he contemplated erecting, was a church,

for which he had selected what he considered an eligible situation.

"The natives were all the time so very friendly, that we were not in the least afraid of them. A great many of them came to our tent every day, and some of them were there day and night, eating, drinking, and sleeping with us. Paine had a girl that he brought from another islet, who did not like to stay with us, and would run away whenever she got an opportunity; he fired muskets at her several times, and at last, used to keep her by putting her in irons.

A few days after the ship ran away, some of the natives, who had been at the tent, stole from us a number of tools. Paine gave four or five of our people muskets without cartridges, and sent them to the natives, a great many of whom were assembled not far off, for the stolen articles. The natives refused to give them up, and soon began to throw stones at our people, who, knowing that they had not the means of resisting, began to retreat; the natives pursued them, throwing stones, and one of the party, Rowland Jones, either fell or was knocked down by his pursuers, who came up immediately afterwards and killed him. When the party returned to the tent, Paine, who had taken the command after Comstock's death, ordered all the muskets brought to him, and locked them up. We were all in or about the tent, when a few hours afterwards the natives came there as usual, but in greater numbers. • After they had been there a little while, some one remarked, ' I am afraid they are going to kill us; they have all got spears, or stones, or sticks in their hands.' Upon this, Paine said he believed we were all taken, but that he was safe. The words were scarcely out of his mouth, when the natives commenced the massacre, knocking our people on the head with stones and clubs, and sticking spears in them. An old man and his wife laid hold of me, one on each side, and led me a little way off in the bushes, where, I thought they were going to kill me, but where they only held me fast and protected me from the violence of several who came and wanted to kill me. I saw two of the natives lead Paine off a little way, and thought they were going to save his life ; but they proceeded only a few yards, when one of them took up a stone and struck him on the head ; he attempted to run, but a second blow brought him down, and they immediately afterwards killed him. Oliver, I did not see ; but the natives told me that he ran a short distance, when he was overtaken and killed in the bushes. A Sandwich Islander that was with us, got to the water, and was overtaken and killed there."

"Were there any women at the massacre?"

"Oh, yes, and children too. The women

seemed to take as active a part as the men. I
saw one old woman run a spear in the back of
one man, who was held by two natives, with a degree of violence that seemed far beyond her
strength. I thought that all but myself were
killed until the following evening. I had been
taken to the islet where your schooner is anchored, and where all the chiefs were assembled,
when they brought Huzzy, to show me that there
was one living besides myself. After an interview of a few hours, Huzzy was taken away to
live with Lugoma, who had saved his life, and I
was taken to live with the old man who had saved
mine. He was so very poor that I scarcely ever
got enough to eat of the coarsest native food. I
had to labour very hard, although I suffered constantly from hunger, which soon made me weak
and extremely wretched. At last, the high chief
took compassion upon me, and made me live with
him; after which, I had always plenty to eat,
and was at liberty to work or not, as I pleased.
He was very kind to me in every respect. They
have always brought Huzzy to me, or taken me
to see him once a fortnight, or once a month, and
suffered us to pass the day together."

Here Lay's narrative ended. Huzzy told us,
that during his residence with Lugoma, his time
had been spent principally on the water, going
with him in his canoe, which required two to work

it. Lugoma was a great fisherman, and distinguished amongst the chiefs for his industry and enterprising character. He would always have enough to eat, if he had to steal it. When Huzzy would complain to him of the hard and laborious life that he led, Lugoma would always reply, that if he would eat he must work. There seems to be no doubt, that the natives saved the lives of these young men from no other motive than that of making them slaves, and availing themselves of the advantage of their labour.

At the dawn of day, we prepared to depart for the schooner, and in getting up our anchor, which was a kedge, weighing upwards of a hundred pounds, we found that it was hooked to a bunch of coral at the bottom, from which all our efforts failed to move it. As soon as Lugoma saw our difficulty, he told his son to go down and clear the anchor. The little fellow jumped into the water, which was about three fathoms deep, and in a few moments came up, making motions for us to haul away. He had disengaged the kedge, and we had no further trouble in getting it up. It is a universal practice amongst the natives, whenever they wish to anchor, to take a line from the end of the canoe, and tie it to a tree of coral at the bottom.

The chief persisted in his desire to leave us, saying he was still afraid I would kill him; and as I had no object in taking him with me against his will, I consented to his departure, presenting him with some seeds, the culture of which I caused to be explained to him, as also the value of the fruit. Our return on board was welcomed by every body. We had now accomplished the object of our visit, and the islands were altogether so void of interest, except for their novel formation, and the singular habits of the natives, that we were well content to leave them and return to some other place more congenial to the feelings of civilized men. Before we left, however, we wished to see the chiefs, and after representing the impropriety of their conduct toward the white men who had sought an asylum upon their islands, point out the course they must in future pursue towards such as might again visit them. On the morning of December the first, none of the chiefs or people residing upon the islet abreast of us having returned, the mother of the high chief was directed to send for her son to come back, and bring with him the rest of the chiefs, without delay. I made a visit to the chief's village, where I found but few inhabitants, most of whom were women and children. It was situated on the side of the island opposite to us, and bordering upon the inland sea. It was not extensive, but a beautiful and romantic spot; the grove of cocoa-nut and bread-fruit trees, through which were scattered the huts of the natives, ran about a hundred yards back from the inland sea to a wild thicket that passes through the centre of the islet, in length two or three hundred yards. Here I found the largest canoe that I had yet seen. It was large enough to carry fifty men, but being old, leaked so badly, that the high chief was compelled to leave it behind, in his flight, with all the rest.

Near the high chief's hut, we came to consecrated ground. It was the place of burial for the royal dead. It was but a small space, comprehended within the circumference of a few yards, and at the head of each grave stood a cocoa-nut tree, bound round with dry leaves,—a mark that prohibited the use of the fruit. We were accompanied by a son of the high chief, a child about twelve years old, who desired us not to tread on the graves of his ancestors. Two graves were pointed out, as those of chiefs, who had been highly distinguished, beside which stood the aged trunks of cocoa-nut trees, that indicated the period of their demise to have been very distant. At one of the huts we saw a domestic fowl, which, when I expressed a wish to purchase, the chief's son, whose name was Ladro, immediately presented me. We afterwards saw a number of others running wild in the thickets. They were small, and looked like what is called the bantam.

The natives never eat them, giving, as the reason for it, that they are not cleanly in their food. On our return, Lay took me to a place, where, after the massacre, he had buried a Spanish dollar. It was still there, and he took it with him as a memento of his captivity. We passed several springs of water, to which the women are banished at a certain period.

We met with a native, whom Lay knew, and who, assuming the native dress, went through the violent motions and gestures of a Mulgrave man, engaged in battle. It was an indescribable mixture of the frightful and ludicrous. I was apprehensive that it would offend the native ; but he laughed with us at the representation, and said, it was very good. On the following morning, December the second, we were disappointed in not seeing the chiefs. The captain went again to the high chief's mother, who made some excuse for their not appearing, and declared, that they would positively be up that night by moonlight. He told her to send to them again, and say, if they were not there on the morrow, he would go after them, and the consequence might be serious. The old woman seemed very much alarmed at hearing such language, and promised a faithful compliance on the part of her son. It had the desired effect, as on the following morning, December the third, the chiefs all presented themselves on the shore,

near our anchorage. The captain, taking Lay
and Huzzy with him, went on shore to meet
them. They told him, by way of opening the
interview, that they were in his power, and ready
to obey all his commands. He required of them
to restore a whale boat that belonged to the
Globe, a swivel, they had taken from the white
men, and Lay's musket, to all of which they
cheerfully assented. He then gave them, as a
proof of his friendship, some cotton handkerchiefs,
axes, and a variety of other articles, of much more
value to them than those he had taken. He told
them, that white men would never come there to
hurt them, and that they must always be kind and
friendly to them, whenever ships should hereafter
visit their island. That, if other white men should
ever be similarly situated to those they had killed,
they must take care of them, and at some future
time they would be rewarded for it. They promised faithfully to do all that they were told, and
regretted having killed our countrymen. We
gave them a pair of pigs, male and female, which
we told them to take great care of, and increase
the number as much as possible, forbidding them,
on pain of our displeasure, to kill any until we
should again return, which might be at no very
distant period, although it was uncertain when.
The surgeon's grave was made a sacred spot by
the high chief, and every thing about it was to be

held in the same reverence as the burial-place of his forefathers. The high chief was instructed, through the interpreters, in the manner of cultivating the fruits and vegetables, the seeds of which we had given him in great variety. Some we planted, and all was to be under his especial care. The use of the various kinds was explained to him, as well as their importance to ships, that might visit his islands, which would give him in return for them, axes, or whatever else was most valuable to him.

On the fourth of December, I obtained a boat, and set off on a visit to Lugoma, who, contrary to his promise, had not yet been on board. I took Huzzy with me, knowing that it would delight the chief to see him. We met with a variety of obstacles in our passage, through the inland sea, and did not arrive at the islet of the chief until the second day after our departure. We stood into his bay in the midst of a heavy shower, notwithstanding which, as soon as he saw us, himself and son ran down to the shore to meet us, and waded up to the middle in the water, extending their arms towards us, full of roasted fish, of which he had taken a large quantity on the preceding day. Both of them called to Huzzy, with repeated expressions of their happiness at seeing him, and, in a moment after we struck the shore, the whobe tribe of old women welcomed us, with

M

their joyful exclamations. As soon as we were
out of the boat, each one in turn clung round
Huzzy's neck, and embraced him in the kindest
manner. In several different huts were large
piles of fish, amounting to some thousands, which
had been roasted to preserve them. Lugoma
offered at once to accommodate us for the night,
saying, he had an abundance of room in his huts
for us to sleep, and plenty of fish for us to eat.
The weather was squally and wet, which induced
me to accept his offer. I wished, also, to witness
the manner in which he caught fish in such quantities, and another opportunity might not offer before I left the islands.

As soon as the shower was over, which lasted
for two or three hours, Lugoma went out, and
employed himself busily collecting and breaking
up dry wood, and arranging his ovens of stones,
that all might be in readiness to cook the fish as
soon they were taken out of the water. There
was a considerable shoal extending out from the
shore, opposite to his huts, upon which the fish, in
their migrations along the islets came in great
numbers. At the outer edge of this shoal he had
sunk, a few feet below the surface of the water,
a long line of cocoa-nut leaves, which were dry,
and of a reddish colour. One end of the line of
leaves was taken to the shore, and made fast,
where there was a pen, built of stone. The line

was then taken round upon the shoal semi-circularly, encompassing a considerable portion of it, and the space between the other end of the line and the shore left quite open. When a school of fish is seen, the natives intercept them, driving them through this open space, and, pressing forward, finally into the stone pen, from which they are taken with nets. After all the arrangements were made, Lugoma and another native, waded out beyond the line of leaves, to watch the schools of fish, but, unfortunately, he allowed them all to escape; and, as well as ourselves, seemed to be a good deal disappointed with his bad success. What appeared to be most remarkable about this method of catching fish, is that, after they are inclosed, they will not pass under the cocoa-nut leaves, although there is a depth of several feet water between them and the bottom. Lugoma took me to the place where he had planted the water-melon seeds, I gave him at the time of our parting. He had cleared and mellowed the ground with care, preparatory to planting the seeds, which were already up, and looked thrifty. I bestowed upon him a great deal of praise, and planted a variety of other seeds, of fruit and vegetables, of which he promised to have an abundant supply for me, when I should again return. When night came, and the hour of repose was at hand, I was perplexed with the difficulty

of providing for our security against surprise or
treachery, without giving Lugoma reason to suppose that we did not confide in his friendship,
which I knew he would infer, from any particular
watchfulness on our part. I did not believe that
we had reason to apprehend danger from Lugoma
or any one else, but as we were exposed to it, and
had the means of security, I was determined not
to run any risk. Three of the men were sent to
sleep in the boat, anchored off a short distance from
the shore, and which Lugoma was told no one
must approach. The rest were directed to bring
their arms on shore, and keep a lookout through
the night, in rotation. When the arrangement
was made, and we had all lain down, except the
man that was standing sentry, Lugoma saw him,
and asked, if there was not room enough for him
to lay down. We answered evasively several
times, with a view to satisfy the uneasiness he
expressed, lest he should be thought wanting in
any respect in hospitality; but were at last
obliged to tell him, that the man was keeping
watch, to see that no one came to hurt us. His
mortification was evident, as he remarked, in reply, that no one would come to his island to hurt
us. We expressed our full confidence in his
friendship, giving him the further information,
that it was our custom always to have some one
on the look-out. Lugoma arranged mats upon

the floors of his huts for us all, and invited me to lay down on one side of him, having his wife and daughter on the other side. It blew and rained hard all night, but the morning was clear and pleasant. We set off on a visit to an islet a few miles beyond that of Lugoma. He offered to go with us, and dive for a large shell-fish, found there; but as we could not take him, without incommoding ourselves, we declined his company. The islet was so uninteresting, as hardly to repay us for the trouble of going to it. It was covered with a thick growth of hard red wood, common to most of the low islands, and wild bup. We soon took our departure from it, and returned to Lugoma's islet, at an early hour of the day.

For the first time, at the Mulgraves', I observed, in one of Lugoma's huts, a drum, resembling those of Nooaheeva, but of small dimensions. I supposed it was an instrument of music, and in compliance with my request, Lugoma readily consented to play on it. Calling his daughter to him, he bade her thump upon it with her hands, whilst he sung, in time with the music, a few short lines, throwing himself in a variety of attitudes, alternately extending one arm, with great vigour, and drawing the other to his breast. Upon inquiring what was the subject of his song, he told me, through Huzzy, that it was the massacre of the white men,—a rudeness, I did not expect,—even from the untutored Lugoma. I declined any further display of his musical powers. When we were preparing to return on board, Lugoma came to me several times, saying, that I might just as well cut his throat, as to take Huzzy away from him. " I have no one," said he, with a distressed look, " that is equally capable of assisting me, to work my canoe, and now, he is going away with his musket, my enemies can come and kill me." Finding, at last, that he could not prevail upon us to leave Huzzy, he said, we must bring him back very soon. That, if we were long absent, we should not find him living. He said, that we must bring him clothes, like ours; guns and axes; and that we should share the government of his islet with him, promising to have an abundant supply for us, of all the fruits and vegetables we had planted.

When he and the old women had taken an affectionate leave of Huzzy, he requested me to take two or three females in my boat, with their baskets of fish, which were intended as a present to the high chief, and land them upon the islet where he lived. We consented to do so, and, after landing them, arrived on board late in the afternoon, the schooner having run down to the Globe's anchorage, where she was now lying.

On the following morning Lugoma made his appearance on the beach, with his little son, having landed with his canoe upon the opposite side of the narrow islet. A boat was sent to bring them off. The chief stared wildly round, astonished, and wondering at every thing he saw. He was very timid, and, notwithstanding our kind reception, appeared to feel extremely doubtful of his safety. His confidence was in a measure gained, however, when we gave him an axe, a piece of cotton handkerchiefs, and some other trifles; and he left us, reminding me of my promise to return. Not long after his departure we got underway, and ran back to the residence of the chiefs, where, at ten, A. M., we came to in our old anchorage.

The captain went on shore, and at two, P. M., December the eighth, returned on board with the high chief, and two others. They were shown every thing about the deck, but without awakening much apparent curiosity. We then beat to quarters, and let them see what a formidable appearance we made, arrayed for battle,—an appearance, truly ridiculous to one accustomed to the imposing effect of a fine ship of war, and calculated to excite our risibility, notwithstanding the seeming gravity we assumed for the occasion. The captain asked the high chief, if he did not wish to hear one of the cannon fired, to which he answered evasively, unwilling, I suppose, to acknowledge his fears, as he had been a great warrior in his time. The captain then told him, that he would have one of them fired, if he was not afraid, which brought the chief to a confession, that he dared not hear it. The chiefs brought a number of presents for the Tamon,* as they called the captain, consisting principally of mats.

When they became tired of remaining on board, and expressed a wish to be sent on shore, we gratified them, and got underway. The high chief's son, who had visited me a number of times before, and to whom I had made presents of trifling value, but important to him, came on board with his father, and expressed a wish to go with me. His father gave his consent, being perfectly willing that he should go; but as there was great probability an opportunity would never offer for him to return, I thought it would be cruel to take him from his native islands, where, in his father's inheritance, he would be so well provided for.

It was late in the evening when we got underway, at the Mulgraves, for the last time. We had surveyed all that part of the islands intervening between our first anchorage and the Globe's landing, and now steered to the eastward by the bearings we had previously taken. Squalls of wind and heavy rain coming on, we soon lost sight of the land. The loud roaring of the surf, off the extreme north-eastern point, as well as the heavy

* Tamon, High Chief.

swell that set in immediately afterwards, apprised us that we had cleared the group. The land was in sight from the mast-head, in the morning, when we ran down for the eastern end of the island, where we had first anchored, and at a convenient distance run along upon the weather side, taking bearings at the end of every base of three or four miles. Near the centre of the windward part of the group we passed a wide opening into the inland sea, not far from which was a reef of considerable extent, where a very high surf was breaking. Within a short distance of the reef, we saw the bottom plainly in ten fathoms water. There was no place on the weather side of the islands, where it was possible to land with any degree of safety. After passing the extreme northern point we steered off, with the trending of the land W. by S. ; and, at sun-down, were up with the island, from whence I had taken Lay, having sailed nearly round the group. Here we hove to for the night.

The group of Mulgrave Islands, as they are called, form a circular chain of narrow strips of land, which are no where more than half a mile wide, inclosing within the circle an inland sea, one hundred and forty miles in circumference, filled with shoals and reefs of coral. It is every where bounded on the sea-side by a bank of coral, that protects it from the violence of the ocean. This bank generally extends but a short distance from

the shore, when it goes off into unfathomable water.
At the chief's islet, where we buried the surgeon,
it was wider than at any other place about the
group, being upwards of a cable's length, which,
for a low coral island, may be considered good
anchorage.   The whole circle is broken alternately into clumps, a few feet above the water, of
level and low coral reefs, some of which are above
high-water mark, and some sufficiently low to
afford a passage for boats.   The clumps vary in
length, but none of them are more than two miles
long, without an interruption of a dry or drowned
reef.   They are covered with a thick growth of
bushes, and trees of small size, except where the
cocoa-nut and bread-fruit trees rear their tall
heads, and wide-spreading branches.   Wherever
these grow, the underwood disappears, and the
place has the appearance of an old forest, cleared
for a pleasure ground, where a few trees have
been left standing, for the advantage of their
shade.

The bread-fruit tree is of two kinds.   One is
the same as that, which is found at the Society,
Sandwich, and many other islands of the Pacific.
This has no seed, and can only be produced by
cuttings from the tree, or shoots, that spring up
from the roots.   The other kind is seminal, and
very much superior to the first.   It was not the
bread-fruit season, when we were at the Mul-

graves, and much to our regret, we could not obtain any of the seeds of this rare and valuable plant. This tree, in general, attains a size considerably larger than that of the common bread-fruit. The leaf of the bread-fruit tree strongly resembles that of the fig, and any one, who has seen the latter, would immediately recognise it, by the resemblance, and the fine rich foliage it bears, when growing luxuriantly. This is by far the most important production of the Mulgrave Islands. When the fruit is not blasted, as sometimes happens, there is a great plenty for the inhabitants. It lasts, however, only for a few weeks; and it is to be presumed, that the natives have no way of preserving it, in a dried or baked state, as is practised with many of the South Sea Islanders, none having been seen by us during our stay. The cocoa-nut tree is next in value to the natives. Of this food there is an ample supply, unless the fruit is blasted. When the bread-fruit and cocoa-nut, both fail in the same year, the natives experience great distress, and are reduced to the necessity of living upon a fruit, they call bup. It is commonly used by the poorest people, and in small quantities by the chiefs at all times. It grows upon almost all the islands in the West Pacific; but, when wild, is much inferior to that growing on the trees, which have a clear open space around them.

Lay lived upon the wild bup for a considerable time after the massacre, when residing with the poor old man, who saved his life, and before the high chief took compassion on him. It has a sweet taste, like the juice of a green corn-stalk. Bread-fruit, cocoa-nuts, and bup, is the only food of the inhabitants of the Mulgrave Islands, except at the season of the year, when great numbers of fish are taken. The industrious and enterprising have an abundant supply at that period; but it is only whilst the season lasts, as they are not in the practice of preserving them. The bup-tree is the most remarkable of all the vegetable productions of the Mulgrave Islands. To shipwrecked seamen, it might be the means of sustaining life, when no other food could be found, and, as it is a never-failing resource, it ought to be generally known amongst those, who navigate the Pacific Ocean. The tree generally grows from twenty to thirty feet high,—sometimes singly, but more frequently in small clusters. The diameter of the body rarely exceeds six inches. It has a hard thick bark, but the wood is spongy, like that of the cocoa-nut tree. It stands on from half a dozen to a dozen roots or prongs, by which it is propped up two or three feet from the ground. The fruit is an exact resemblance of a pine-apple. Its smell, when ripe, is at first agreeable, but, so powerful, that it soon becomes offensive. The

taste of the ripe fruit has much the same effect—
agreeable at first, like a mellow, sweet apple, but
cloying and nauseous to the stomach, when taken
in any quantity. The ripe fruit is never eaten by
the natives of the Mulgraves. When green, it is
not considered in a state to be eaten, until a
beard, which grows out alongside of the stem, has
acquired a length of four or five inches. It may
then be taken from the tree, and eaten raw, or
roasted between hot stones. The soft part of
the seeds (if I may so call them) is alone palatable, the other part being hard and tough. The
manner of eating it is, to twist the soft part off
with the teeth, whereby the juice is expressed.
There was but little about the islands that would
excite the interest of either the botanist or natu-
ralist. We saw but few flowers or plants. The
islands were swarming with a species of small
rat, that had a tuft of hair upon its tail. The
natives spoke of them as being very troublesome.
By throwing a small quantity of food upon the
ground, near one of the huts, dozens of them
could be collected together in a few moments.

When one of the natives is sick, the friends
collect at the hut, where he is lying, and chant
over him, to appease the offended spirit that has
afflicted him. The same prescription is given for
all diseases, which is a tea, made from an herb
found upon the island. If death takes place, the

friends of the deceased assemble, and mourn over the body, keeping it until it becomes very offensive. Frequently, in the midst of their most bitter mourning and lamentation, some of the mourners will intentionally say or do something calculated to excite mirth, when they all burst out into immoderate laughter, as if their mourning were the affectation of children, and as soon as the humorous excitement has passed over, again relapse into their mournful strain of howling and chaunting. When the body can be kept no longer, and the day of interment arrives, the grave is dug, and the corpse taken upon sticks, and carried to it by the friends of the deceased, followed by a large concourse, who move along without order, and some one occasionally breaks in upon their solemnity by a humorous trick, which gives rise to others, and sets them all laughing. This is soon again succeeded by mourning. The body is lowered into the grave, and covered up, when a little canoe, with a sail to it, and laden with small pieces of cocoa-nut or other food, having been previously prepared, is taken to the sea-shore on the leeward part of the island, and sent off, with a fair wind, to bear far away from the island the spirit of the deceased, that it may not afterwards disturb the living. This ceremony is considered indispensably necessary, and is never neglected. At the head of the grave a cocoa-nut is planted, the tree that springs from which, is held sacred, and its fruits never eaten, in times of the greatest famine. Their burial places are usually a short distance back of the houses, and the females are strictly prohibited from going to them.

Their marriages are conducted with but little ceremony. If a man fancies a female for his wife, he makes the proposal to her, which, if agreeable, he applies to her friends. They meet, and hold a consultation, as to the propriety of the match, and decide whether it shall take place. If the man's suit is denied, nothing more is said on the subject. When united, they are said to be very faithful, and jealous of each other's chastity. Lay or Huzzy related an occurrence, that took place during their residence on the islands, which shows how keenly a sense of injury is felt by them, and that jealousy sometimes inspires them with the most ferocious and deadly revenge. A young man had taken a young woman for a wife, whom he supposed to be a virgin. In a very short time after she went to live with him, however, it was evident that she was pregnant, and before the period which nature has prescribed had elapsed, gave birth to a child. The indignant husband took the infant from its mother's arms, and in her presence dashed its head upon a stone in front of his hut. It was an act for which, under other circumstances, he would have suffered death, by a custom of the islands, forbidding the destroying of human life ; and, as the female was of superior rank to the man, being the daughter of a chief, it was believed that he would be punished. Her friends were loud in their calls for justice upon the offender, until a council of the chiefs was called, and the matter brought before them.

After an investigation, the chiefs were satisfied, that the woman had grossly imposed upon her husband, whom they suffered to depart without censure. It is permitted to the men to have as many wives as they can get ; but as food is very scarce, and they find it difficult to support one, there are few, even of the chiefs, who have more. The high chief was the only exception to this remark at the time of our visit. He had six, one of whom was a particular favourite.

Latuano, the high chief of the Mulgraves, was called the greatest warrior that the islands had produced for a long time. He told us that in one of his wars he was driven from his islands, and remained (I think) fourteen days at sea in his canoe, most of the time out of sight of land. He steered for an island, which, according to the tradition of his countrymen, lay to the west of the Mulgraves, and, after a great deal of suffering, arrived there in safety. The high chief of this

isle (south Pedder's Island) received him with
kindness, and after he had visited thirteen different islands of the group,* sent him back to the
Mulgraves with a fleet of canoes, and a great
many men. He arrived there in safety, conquered his enemies, and at the time of our visit
was tributary to the chief of Pedder's Island, who
had given him a daughter or grand-daughter in
marriage. They told us that every few years
the chief of Pedder's Island, who is very powerful
and very wise, sends a fleet of canoes to the Mulgraves, for tribute. Lay and Huzzy were to
have been sent to him, as also the Globe's whale-
boat and swivel. I was particularly struck with
Latuanos' strong resemblance to General Bolivar.
His stature was about the same, and his face bore
the same marks of care and serious thought, when
his attention was not awakened to any particular
thing; and, when animated by conversation, the
same vivid expression beamed from his fine features, and sparkling black eyes. I could not but
think, when I was looking at him, that if he and
General Bolivar could be placed near to each
other, similarly dressed, it would be difficult to
tell which was the Indian chief, and which the
patriot hero.

The high chief is absolute in his authority, but,
in the administration of justice, particularly where

* Called the Reef Chain Tide Islands.

N

the life of an individual is concerned, he is influenced in passing judgment by the opinion of the chiefs of most consequence.* Like all other men, whether civilized or uncivilized, they have different grades of rank in their society, from the high chief down to the farthest remove of relationship to royalty. The different islets that are inhabited, are partitioned off to different chiefs, who acknowledge their subordination to the high chief, by sending him a part of whatever grows, or is taken within the limits of their government. They send him a portion of their cocoa-nuts, bread-fruit, and bup, and of the fish or birds, that may be caught by themselves or any of their people. The high chief requires this for the support of his numerous family. Besides his wives and children, he usually keeps a large number of men about him, who ·go in his canoe, and perform other essential duties in his service. Several of the principal chiefs are also in attendance, and live with him constantly. In his family, there

---

* Lay witnessed the execution of a man during his residence at the Mulgraves. I do not remember the nature of his offence. He was not bound, or in any way confined; bu , after it was determined that he should die, several men attacked him with spears and stones. He fought desperately to the last; although his situation was altogether hopeless, freely bestowing upon his enemies the epithets of cowards and murderers. Even when he could no longer resist, his spirit was unconquered,—and he breathed his last, with expressions of scorn and hatred on his lips.

is no ceremony, to remind the common people of their lowly condition. They all eat, drink, and sleep alike. In dress, there is nothing to distinguish the chiefs from the common people, except that the former sometimes wear a mat that comes down to the knee, of straw, and finely wrought. This, however, I believe, is only worn upon particular occasions.

The men wear bunches of grass hanging down before and behind, such as I have described at our first anchorage, being about the size and appearance of a horse's tail. Those in most common use, were of a reddish colour; but a few of them were white. The bark of which they are made is taken from a long running vine. The boys go quite naked until they are ten or twelve years old, when a dress similar to that of the men is put on them. Their ornaments consist of shell bracelets and necklaces, and sometimes a string of them is put round the head; flowers, when they can be obtained, are often used instead of shells. Many of the men, and some of the women have large slits in their ears, through which they put rolls of leaves from one to two inches in diameter. The women wear beautiful white straw mats, of elegant workmanship, about two feet square, and sometimes larger, bordered round the edge, from one to two inches, with black diamond figures, worked in with coloured straw, died with the husk of the cocoa-nut. They usually wear two of these mats, one of which is behind and the other before, tied round the waist with a beautiful round cord of braided straw. The ornaments of the women are the same as those worn by the men.

They have no manner of worship. They acknowledge the existence of a Great Spirit whom they call Kenneet, and who, they say, can make them sick and kill them: they look for nothing good from him, and, so far as I could learn, have no idea of rewards and punishments after death.

They have a sort of conjurers amongst them, for whose art they entertain great reverence, and in whom they place a strict reliance. To them they apply in all cases of great emergency. Their art consists in having a large bunch of straws, which they fold double and tie in a great many different ways; if, after the straws are thus folded, doubled, and tied, they can be drawn out without being in any manner entangled the one with the other, the omen is propitious; but otherwise, the contemplated undertaking is relinquished. On the following morning it is again resorted to, and so on until success is promised. It must never be tried but in the morning, and only once on the same day. The morning I took Lay from the natives, the chiefs had recourse to this art before they would allow him to speak to us; they were promised good fortune, otherwise he

would have been concealed from us.   He who
cannot perform the mysteries of this art, is not allowed to drink from the same cup with him who
can.

They had a great aversion to hearing us whistle, particularly in their houses, and would invariably run up to any of our people when they
were whistling, and with a fearful look, beg them
to stop ; saying, it would bring spirits about the
house that would make them sick and kill them.
If one of them has wronged another who has died,
or if they were enemies, he never eats without
throwing away a portion* of his food to appease
the ghost of the departed.

At a meeting we had with the chiefs on shore,
the captain remarked an old man in the circle,
whose name and character he asked of Lay or
Huzzy ; being replied to, he said, in a stern manner that he did not like his face, meaning that
he looked like a bad man.   The old fellow, seeing himself the subject of conversation, asked the
interpreter what the captain was saying about
him.   On being told, his countenance expressed
the utmost dismay, and in a day or two afterwards, he died.   There was not a native on the
islands with whom Lay or Huzzy conversed, that

---

* Lay frequently saw the people, who performed the execution
I have mentioned in a former note, throw away portions of their
food, as an offering to the spirit of him they had slain.

did not believe the captain's dislike killed the old man. They seemed to entertain the most singular notions of the captain's supernatural powers.

For the purpose of ascertaining what idea the high chief entertained of a God, the captain asked him several questions, to which his answers were vague and unsatisfactory. He thought he had conceived the right one, when he asked the chief who he thought made it thunder. After a moment's hesitation, he looked at the captain and replied, " I suppose you can make it thunder." This was as satisfactory as any thing he could be made to express. Thunder he believed was produced by the agency of a being superior to himself, and the captain he conceived to be infinitely his superior.

Not long after the massacre of the white men, the natives were visited by a disease that caused their limbs to swell, and produced great distress amongst them ; it was before unknown, and they ascribed it to Lay and Huzzy, who, they believed, had the power to afflict them in that manner, and had done it to be revenged for the death of their countrymen. They finally charged them with it, and threatened to kill them, which, in all probability they would have done, but for their superstitious fear of some greater evil.

Their huts are not, generally, more than ten by fifteen feet, and from ten to fifteen feet high.

They are divided into two apartments, upper and lower; the lower is open all round, without any thatching; the floor is raised a little above the adjacent ground, and covered over with small pieces of the cleanest and whitest coral that can be found. The rafters and small sticks that are laid across them for the thatching, are secured by twine made from the outer husk of cocoa-nut, with which the thatching is also secured. The thatch is the leaves of palm or cocoa-nut. The ceiling of the lower room is generally so low, that one must bend almost double to get into it, and if you remain, it must be in a lying or sitting posture. The garret has a floor of sticks thickly interwoven with leaves; it is higher than the ground floor, and has an air of comfort. The natives keep their provisions in it, and all such things as they would preserve from the rats. They also sleep there in wet weather. In the floor, a hole is left just large enough for a person to crawl through, and so far from the sides that the rats cannot get to it.

Their canoes display the greatest ingenuity, and I have no doubt, that in a civilized country, they would be ranked amongst the rarest specimens of human industry, unassisted but by the rudest implements. The model is most singular, and differs from all that I have ever seen in use, either in the European or American world. Its construction is so remarkable, and in many respects so inconvenient, that it seems improbable the model should have had its origin in any other cause than the want of suitable timber for a more perfect structure. The depth of a Mulgrave canoe, of common size, is four or five feet; its length from thirty to forty. It is so narrow that a man can scarcely stand in it; perfectly flat on one side, and round on the other. It is sharp at both ends. The mast is from twelve to twenty-five feet long, and the sail, (a straw mat,) which is bent to a small yard, is very large in proportion to the canoe. They always sail on the flat side, and have the mast a little inclined forward. It is supported by shrouds and a guy at either end, which is used at pleasure to give the mast its proper inclination. In beating to windward, instead of tacking as we do, and presenting the other side of the boat to the wind, they bring the other end of the boat to it, making that the bow which was before the stern. Amidships there are several light spars extending about ten feet over the round side, and four over the other. Across these are smaller sticks, which are securely lashed above and below, and over them is made a platform. Upon that part of it which extends over the flat side, they have a small thatched cabin, in which they store whatever they wish to preserve from getting wet, or would conceal from observation.

The other part of the platform is intended to keep
the canoe from being upset ; and when hard pressed with carrying sail, several men will sometimes
get on it, to keep the canoe upright. They move
through the water with astonishing velocity, and,
in turning to windward, no boats can surpass
them. Although the natives had no other tools
to work with than what they made of shells, previous to the visit of the Globe, every article of
their workmanship is neat, and as highly polished
as though it had been wrought with steel. In the
construction of their canoes, the keel-stern and
sternpost are solid pieces of hard wood, upon which
they are built up of small pieces laid one above the
other, and closely seized on with the line of co-
coa-husk. The seams are neither caulked or pay-
ed, and the canoe consequently leaks so much as
to require one man to bail constantly. The steer-
age is very laborious ; they have no rudder, and
the only means by which they steer, is with a
long flat paddle held in the hands of the helmsman.
To steer a large canoe in blowing weather, requires the utmost strength of six or eight men.
Upon the outriggers or platforms, and along the
masts, they arrange their spears, which are always taken with them, even upon the most ordinary occasions. The canoes are also always bal-
lasted with a quantity of round stones, weighing
about a pound each, which forms a material part

of their armament. Our carpenter was several days at work upon the canoe of the high chief, caulking and graving her. When he had completed his work, the high chief, after expressing his gratification, earnestly solicited the captain to leave him on the island; he said that he would always provide him an abundance to eat, and that no one should ever hurt him. This, according to the high chief's standard, was the most ample reward that he could promise for useful services.

The people of the Mulgraves are in general of moderate stature, and well made. Their complexion is not so dark as that of the natives of the Duke of Clarence and Byron's Island, and their features more comely. They appeared to us like a different race of men. They have not the flat noses and thick lips of the low islanders, except that two or three persons we saw would come under that description. Their hair is long and invariably combed out with great neatness, and tied on the top of their heads. Their deportment is modest and manly, and after one becomes a little accustomed to their dress, they have always an air of gentility. They have a fine majestic walk, which one would hardly suppose, when it is considered that their way is everywhere paved with sharp coral.

After we had given them the pigs, it was amusing to see with what apparent pleasure they car-

ried them about in their arms, nursing them with
as much care and tenderness, as though they had
been children, whilst the pigs, unused to such
treatment, were kicking and scratching the naked
bodies of the poor natives, and squealing away
most lustily. We had to interfere to keep the
pigs from being killed with kindness, and finally
prevailed upon the chief to forbid their being pet-
ted in this style. It is not improbable that, in a
few years, the whalers that may have occasion
to cruise in the vicinity of these islands, will find
an abundant supply. It is hoped, however, that
until they become numerous, no navigator who
may chance to touch there, will encourage the
natives to diminish their number.

At 4, A. M., on the 9th of December, we took
our departure from the Mulgrave Islands, and
stood to the westward. At daylight, we had lost
sight of the group, and at 10, A. M., made South
Pedder's Island. Having stood a little too far to
the southward, we were all day beating up to
weather the N. E. point, where, at sun-down, we
hove to in the hope that on the following morning
we should be able to effect a landing, and get a
sight of the great chief, so celebrated amongst the
people we had just left. On the 11th of December, having passed all the early part of the day
searching in vain for anchorage, we hove to, a
little after meridian, opposite to a considerable

bay, upon the shore of which was a native village, and large forests of cocoa-nut trees. The captain took Huzzy in the gig, and, followed by another boat, pulled in over a wide coral bank to the village. A few people were attracted to the shore by the appearance of our boats. They immediately conducted the captain to the chief, who was seated on a mat in the open air, in front of his hut. He seemed but little moved at the unexpected appearance of his visitors. He was a very old man, and had a long white beard that came down upon his breast. The natives stood round in respectful silence, as the old chief addressed the captain, whom he soon distinguished as the person of highest rank amongst the strangers. He spoke the same language as the inhabitants of the Mulgraves, and Huzzy was forbidden to let him know that he was understood, but to listen attentively to what he was saying to those around him. For a time his intercourse with the captain was carried on by signs, and Huzzy overheard him say to the natives, standing by, "Don't disturb them yet. Wait until to-morrow, and see what they are going to do. They will look round here to see what they can find, trade a little, and go on board of their vessel, to sleep, and to-morrow they will come again." When the captain told Huzzy to address some questions to the chief in his own language, it seemed to operate as quickly as an electric shock upon the natives, who stared wildly around at him, and at each other, with looks of the utmost astonishment. The chief partially lost his gravity in the sensation it produced, being not less surprised than his subjects. He asked Huzzy, before answering the question put to him, where he had learned to speak the language of Pedder's Island. Huzzy replied, that he had learned it at the Mulgrave Islands, where he had been for two years. The old chief said, that he had been informed of two white men being there, and was then fitting out a fleet of canoes to send after them. He expressed a great deal of disappointment, that we had taken them away, saying, he would have had them brought to his own island, and treated them well. He asked, if Lay was also on board of the vessel. The captain had taken on shore a present for the chief, and a number of trifles, that he thought might be acceptable to the natives. Our people endeavoured to obtain a quantity of cocoa-nuts and bup, of which there was the greatest abundance; but the natives parted with their fruit very reluctantly. When finally the captain addressed the chief, upon the subject of giving or selling us a supply, he said,—No! that his island was thickly inhabited, and produced no more food than was necessary for his people. That, if we were in want of cocoa-nuts and bup, there were other islands, not far to the westward, where there was an abundance, and but few people, and he advised our going there as speedily as possible. Upon being asked, if he had ever seen white men before, he replied,—Yes; that a long time ago there came a large vessel, in which there were white men, who brought their forge on shore, where they remained for several days. This, he said, was the only instance. The young women were all sent away, and concealed in the thickets, or upon a distant part of the island, where they remained during the whole day.

Amongst other presents made by the captain to the high chief, was a battle-axe,—to him an article of the greatest value. He received it, however, with reluctance, expressing his regret, that he had it not in his power to make a suitable return for so valuable a consideration, accompanying his apology with a small present of mats, cocoa-nuts, and a preparation of the ripe bup, that had an agreeable sweet taste. It was after dark when our party left the village, and went to the beach to embark. They had already left the shore a few yards, when some natives came running down, and called for them to return, saying, the chief had another mat for the captain. They landed, when they were told, that the mat was in the village, and that Huzzy must go for it. The captain, not choosing to send for the mat, put off again. In a few moments two or three other messengers came running to the beach, calling for the boat to return. When she had pulled in a few yards from the shore, they said that the chief wanted Huzzy to go up to the village for the mat, and that he did not wish to keep the axe, which he had sent back to the captain, unwilling, as we supposed, to lay himself under so great an obligation as its acceptance implied. The captain refused to take the axe, telling the messenger to say to his chief, that what we had given, we never took back, and, with this, left the shore and returned on board. The tide had risen considerably over the coral bank, and the party found the surf somewhat dangerous in returning, having their boats nearly filled with water.

The dress and general appearance of these people, as well as their language, was the same as that of the natives of the Mulgraves. Their canoes were also the same. We saw only three or four with sails, which were hauled upon the beach. The power of the great chief must, therefore, consist in his dominion over other islands to the northward and westward of him, where there is an almost connected chain for several hundred miles, and from which, when he undertakes an important enterprise, he must, in a great measure, draw his resources. It was probably with the object of collecting forces for the great chief, that Latuano visited so many islands during his exile from his own, and to which he was at last restored by foreign aid.

At eight in the evening, we made sail to the northward and westward, with a fresh breeze from the eastward. The weather was clear, and we stood on under easy sail all night. Early in the morning land was discovered, bearing nearly west, and soon afterwards more land was seen to the north. The last was Ibbitson's Island, and appeared to be separate from that discovered first. It is not improbable, however, that they are connected by coral reefs, that were too distant from us to be observed.

The land was all low, and had the appearance of the Mulgraves and other coral islands. At meridian, we hove to, and put off in two boats. Having passed to leeward of the island, we crossed a drowned reef, that extended as far as the eye could reach to the N. W., when we found ourselves in an inland sea, which was extensive and quite smooth. That part of the island where we landed was about five miles long, and a quarter of a mile wide. Upon the margin of the inland sea, there were a number of huts, but when we landed, not an inhabitant could be seen. The huts had evidently been but recently occupied. The island was covered abundantly with cocoanut and bup trees, and a few of the bread-fruit

were here and there to be seen. On the shore of
the inland sea the water was smooth and unruf-
fled, and the humble but neat dwellings of the
natives, scattered about amongst the cocoa
forests, presented a scene of quiet and repose,
peculiarly soothing to the mind, contrasted with
the eternal war of breakers on the ocean side.
We had not been long on shore before we found a
few old people, who had concealed themselves in
the bushes, and, although they were at first afraid
of us, they became less timid, and increased in
number, when we had presented them with some
pieces of iron, and a few old buttons. In return,
they gave us mats, fishing-nets, cocoa-nuts, and
bup, with the last of which they filled our boat.
Their dress and language was the same as at the
Mulgraves, and their habitations and canoes were
also the same. Amongst all these islands, the
natives ascend the cocoa-nut trees, in the way I
have described at the Marquesas. Here we saw
several very old people, some of whom had lost
all their teeth,—a circumstance we had not before
remarked in any of these islands. There were
also two or three cripples, who were not less remarkable, being the first we had seen. All the
females were very old, and, upon inquiring the
cause, they replied, that the young men had sent
the young women away, for fear they would be
given presents. Two or three large sail canoes

o

came from a great distance over the inland sea, and approached us without fear. The natives told us that they had never seen white men before.

The captain landed upon a different island from myself, and the natives, having fled from their habitations as they did upon the island where I landed, he sent a few old people, that were found, commanding all the inhabitants to return to their homes, and, fearing his displeasure, in a few minutes their huts were occupied in the same manner as though the white-faced strangers had not appeared amongst them.

At five, P. M., we returned to the schooner, with our boats laden with fruit, and soon afterwards made sail, shaping our course for the Sandwich Islands. We were favoured with south easterly trades, blowing in fresh gales for a number of days, which rendered our passage materially shorter than it would probably have been otherwise. But what was still less to have been expected than a south-east trade in the northern tropic, was a strong current, that set us at the rate of thirty to forty miles a day, N. E. from the latitude of sixteen to twenty-five north. Part of the time that we experienced this strong current, the wind was blowing a double-reefed top-sail breeze from East and E. N. E., differing only from two to four points with the opposite direction of the current. When we arrived in the latitude of twenty-three degrees north, the trades left us, and the winds became variable. At meridian of December the 24th, we were, by our calculation, thirty miles from an island, said to have been discovered recently by a whaler, and which we made to bear from us E. by N. Our latitude observed was twenty-five degrees fifty-seven minutes, N. Longitude, by chronometer, one hundred and eighty-six degrees twenty-seven minutes, W. We ran off to the eastward all the following day, and at meridian, December 25th, observed, in latitude twenty-six degrees, N.; longitude one hundred and eighty-three degrees twenty minutes W., without having seen the slightest indications of land.

On Christmas day, we gave the crew a dinner of turtle, which were still fat, and very delicious. We had fed them occasionally upon bup and other vegetation, that was found upon the islands.

December the 27th, we came within the vicinity of another new discovery of a whaler, and at meridian, had it bearing, by our calculation, S. E. ten miles. We ran for it until six, P. M., December 28th, when no appearance of land being in sight, we hove about, and stood to the northward, for a newly discovered reef, which, at meridian, bore from us, by calculation N. by E., distant one hundred miles. Latitude observed,

twenty-six degrees ten minutes N. ; longitude, by
chronometer, one hundred and seventy-six degrees
fifty-one minutes, W. The reef for which we
were now steering was called, by the discoverer,
Clark's Reef. It was said to extend sixty miles,
in a south-west and north-easterly direction, and
we thought it impossible that it should escape our
observation, if laid down any where near the given
latitude and longitude.

At nine, P. M., December the 30th, we were
within twenty-five miles of the centre of the reef,
by our calculation, and as it was blowing a gale,
and we were scudding before it with an unusually
high sea, we hove to for the night. At three,
A. M., we again made sail, and ran for the centre
of the reef. At meridian, December the 31st, the
centre of it was still twenty miles from us, bearing N. E. by N. From meridian to one, P. M.,
we steered N. by E., and then bore up, and
steered east all the rest of the twenty-four hours,
without seeing the reef or any indications of it. At
meridian, observed, in latitude twenty-six degrees
forty-seven minutes, N. ; longitude, by chronometer, one hundred and seventy-two degrees
eleven minutes, W.

We continued on to the eastward, with the hope
of falling in with two islands and a reef, of another
whaler's discovery. Our confidence in their
given latitude and longitude, however, was quite

destroyed by frequent disappointments, and we now looked for their discoveries, as we would have sought for lands, known only in the tradition of the natives of some unfrequented island, with the hope of finding them, but with little expectation of success. It happened with these, as with all the rest of the new discoveries we had looked for. We passed within a few miles of the latitude, and ran down from one to two degrees of longitude, without observing any thing that indicated the vicinity of land.

On the second of January, 1826, we ran off to the southward of east for Ballard's Island. During the middle of the day, the sea, from being very heavy, became comparatively smooth, and continued so for sixty miles, when the heavy swell again set in from the westward, as before.

At three, P. M., on the fourth of January, a rock was reported from the mast-head, eight leagues from us. It proved to be Ballard's Island, as it is called. At eight on the following morning, we passed within two hundred yards of it. It is about two or three hundred yards in circumference, and rises two hundred feet from the sea. On one side it has a considerable inclination, where seals had crawled up, and several were basking in the sun, almost to the very top. Large flocks of birds were perched upon its ragged sides, or wending their flight around it. Not the least sign of vegetation was any where to be seen. Near its base, was a small rock, from ten to twenty feet above the water level. Ballard's Rock rises in three equi-distant peaks, the centre of which is the highest, and all of them, to the very base, are white with bird-lime. A high surf breaks all around it. Our observations placed it in north latitude, twenty-five degrees two minutes ; west longitude, one hundred and sixty-seven degrees fifty minutes.

On the evening of January the fifth, the weather became squally, with constant flashes of lightning and distant thunder. From south to west, and N. W., the heavens were obscured with a heavy black cloud, which rose with great rapidity. We furled all sail. When the cloud ascended our zenith, it became perfectly calm, and a roaring was heard in the air for several minutes, like that of wind through the tops of pines, when hail-stones of an unusual size began to fall upon our deck, accompanied with very sharp lightning and heavy thunder. The hail was of short duration, and passed over without a breath of wind.

The nearest of the Sandwich Group was Bird Island, for which we steered, and on the ninth of January, at eight in the morning (having the preceding night been enveloped in fog it was discovered close to us. We tacked and stood back close in with the south-west side, where was a small sand-beach, fifty to a hundred yards long.

The captain, taking the Globe's whale-boat, went in shore to fish, but seeing a few seal upon the sand beach, was induced to land. It soon afterwards became squally and blew with great violence. The surf upon the beach rose with the wind, and, when the captain, after a short examination of the island, attempted to return, he found it impossible to launch his boat through the surf, and was reduced to the necessity of passing the night upon the island. It blew a gale and rained in torrents all night. The captain and his boat's crew took shelter in a cavern upon the sea-shore, where they had not been long by a comfortable fire they had made, when, by the rising of the tide the sea broke in upon them, and they with difficulty escaped to the side of the rocks, and thence upon the sand-beach. The island was high and almost perpendicular, and with the floods that fell and rushed down its steep sides, rocks of a large size were disengaged from their beds, and came tumbling down in every direction, to the great peril of the captain and his boat's crew, sufficiently uncomfortable from the torrents of water that were falling and driving upon the gale. After a little search, they found an asylum in a cave at the side of a mountain, where they passed the night In the morning, when they ascended the

mountain, the schooner was no where to be seen.
It was high and steep, and she had beat up within
a few miles of the island and passed their line of
sight.   Their disappointment and chagrin was
inexpressible, supposing, from the schooner's not
being in sight, she had been driven off, and that it
would be a considerable time before she could return, and afford them that relief their situation so
much required, being very much fatigued and exhausted from their exposure.   At day-light, the
weather cleared and the wind moderated.   We
beat up and hove to off the sand-beach nearly as
soon as the boat we had sent with refreshments.

When the captain saw the schooner approaching close in with the island, he made a last effort
to launch his boat.   They succeeded in getting her
into the breakers, but the first heavy roller that
broke under them severed the boat amid-ships, and
the captain upon one end of her and a man that
could not swim on the other, were hove up safely
on the beach by the succeeding wave.   The rest
of the boat's crew were good swimmers, and also
landed in safety.   Our boat was not far off when
this occurred, and anchoring as near as possible to
the shore, the men, all but one, swam off to her
through the surf.   The only way we could de-
vise to get the captain and seaman off, was to float
a cork-jacket on shore, at the end of a line, which
being put on by the captain and seaman, alter

nately, and a rope tied round them, they were hauled throhgh the surf without any other injury than swallowing a quantity of salt-water.

Bird's Island is an uninhabited rock, about a league in circumference, and the highest part from five to eight hundred feet above the ocean. Where our boat landed, is the only spot where a landing could be effected, and upon that side alone it has an inclination by which it may be ascended. Every where else it is perpendicular, and at a distance, looks like the work of art. It has a scanty vegetation.

At five, P. M., January the 11th, we made sail for the island of Oahoo, with a fine breeze from the westward and pleasant weather. At daylight, on the following morning, we saw the small island of Onehow, and soon afterwards, the highland of Atooi. During the whole day, we were coming up with and sailing along on the west side of Atooi, moving at the rate of eight and nine miles per hour. Of a clear day, it may be seen at least fifty or sixty miles. We did not approach nearer to it than eight or ten. It had the appearance, at that distance, of beautiful tableland, being every where very regular and of nearly the same altitude. Towards evening, on the 12th of January, we made the island of Oahoo, and should have been at anchor in Onavoora on the following day had we passed between Atooi and

Oahoo, but from some mistake about the prevailing winds on the opposite side of Oahoo, we continued on round the north end of it, and did not anchor at Onavoora until the sixteenth. Two or three American merchant vessels were lying there, with which we exchanged salutes. The Dolphin was the first American man-of-war that ever entered a harbour of the Sandwich Islands, and the firing of the guns, and the report widely circulated that an American man-of-war had arrived, brought the inhabitants from far and near to the shore of the harbour to witness the novel sight. Several of our countrymen, who were traders here, and had been expecting us for some time, came on board to offer their congratulations, and invite us on shore to partake of their hospitality. It was highly gratifying to us upon landing, to meet nearly all of our countrymen residing at the Island, who came down, en masse, to the beach, to welcome us on shore, in the most kind and friendly manner. We were a little disappointed, however, when we came to look round and found that none of the missionaries had partaken in the general sentiment. They were also our countrymen, and from the character of benevolence and philanthropy they had assumed to themselves, we had a right to expect they would have been amongst the first to hail us with a welcome to their lonely abode. We expected, in-

deed, that they would not only have received us
as countrymen, but as friends, whose kindness,
and sympathy would be highly acceptable to them
in their peculiar situation.

From the shore we were escorted to a large
frame building called the wooden-house, then occupied by our countryman, Captain Wilds, where
a handsome dinner was prepared, to which every
luxury was added that could be obtained from the
shipping or the shore. We were much surprised
on landing, to find a rabble of naked and half-
naked natives, amounting to many hundreds, as
we had been taught to believe, from the various information we had received, that their condition was much improved, and that they were
far advanced in civilization. They were of all
ages, and formed a more varied and fantastic
group than I had any where seen, even where no
degree of civilization had taken place, from an intercourse with white men. Some of them were
quite naked ; some had their native dress of tappa
cloths ; some had on cotton shirts, some a pair of
old trowsers, and some nothing but an old jacket.
Many of them had adorned their heads with
wreaths of red and yellow flowers, and some their
necks and wrists with necklaces and bracelets of
shells. They expressed the greatest pleasure at
seeing us, shouting and crowding around, so that
we could not get along without pushing them out

of the way. In appearance, a comparison of them
with the natives of the Marquesas or Mulgrave
Islands, would have been greatly to their disadvantage. On the following day, we were again
invited to dine at the same place, where we met a
second time with our countrymen, and interchanged with them those sentiments of friendship and
sympathy that naturally arise on meeting in a
strange land, and which are felt by Americans
with peculiar force. It appeared to us that they
could not sufficiently express their gratification at
seeing us at Oahoo, by the most unremitted attention, for they continued to feast and give us parties
every day for more than a week, and until our
various and pressing duties made it inconvenient
for us to partake of them. On the first sabbath
after our arrival, I went to the place of worship
appointed by the missionaries for the natives. A
large building, formerly occupied for this purpose,
had been destroyed a short time previous to our
arrival, and as they had now no house sufficiently
large to contain the whole congregation, the
place appointed for worship was an extensive enclosure in the rear of a large frame building, which
is occupied as the dwelling of the young king.
Within this enclosure, was assembled about a
thousand people, as I supposed, seated on the
ground. Some of them were dressed in silks,
cottons, and calicoes, and others were in their na-

tive dress, being quite naked, except about the waist. They were in the open air, without any protection from the sun, which was pouring its vertical rays upon them. Mr. Bingham, the head of the mission, was addressing them in the language of the island, and when he saw me at the outer edge of the circle, very kindly beckoned me to come round where the queen dowager was seated. He was standing there himself. A native was holding an umbrella over his head, and around him were seated all the chief men and women, some in chairs, and some of them on the ground. With one or two exceptions, they were all people of uncommon size. Some of them were quite neatly dressed, but others had displayed a most whimsical and ridiculous fancy. When I came near Cahumanu, who was the favourite wife of the departed and highly distinguished Tamahamaha, she extended her hand to me and bade one of her attendants bring me a chair. The service lasted about an hour, when the assemblage dispersed, and the natives ran away as much pleased as so many children let loose from school. At the close of the service, I promised myself so much politeness on the part of the distinguished personages present, as to receive from some of them an invitation to go into their houses, as I was in the uniform of a foreign officer; but in this I was altogether disappointed. I had the satisfaction of speaking, for a few minutes, with Mr. Bingham, whose attention was soon called from me by the presence of some chief, with whom he wished to exchange a salutation, and after recognizing two or three of the chiefs present whom I had seen before, I was suffered to depart without receiving any further notice.

On Monday, I made a call of ceremony on the high chief Boqúe, who was one of the attendants of the late king Rio Rio, on his visit to the king of England. He was a man of about thirty years of age, upwards óf six feet, and stout in proportion. He had a flat nose and thick lips, but the general expression of his face was that of benevolence and good nature—an expression truly characteristic, according to the testimony of those who have had an opportunity of knowing him well. We found him sitting in a chair at a table, with a desk before him, upon which he was making pot-hooks after a copy, having just commenced learning to write. He got up and shook hands with us, as did also his wife, who was seated on some mats at the other end of the hut. Boque was dressed in a coarse linen shirt and trowsers, having a pair of heavy shoes on his feet, without any stockings. Queen Boque was nearly as large as her husband, and looked a good deal like him. She had on a plain white muslin cap and dress, neither of which were very clean or neatly put on. It was, however, in as good taste as could be expected in so rude a state of society, but I thought it less becoming than would have been her native dress. She invited us to be seated, and made an attempt at politeness, such as she had seen practised in England, having accompanied her husband thither. The hut was an oblong building, about sixty by forty feet. Its simple structure was the same that has been in use in the islands from time immemorial, being poles laid over crotches, upon which the rafters rested, and differing in nothing from the habitations of the poorest people, except that the crotches, poles, and rafters, were longer, and there were more of them. It was thatched from the top all the way to the ground, with a thick covering of grass. The interior was all in one apartment, from the top of the rafters to the hard beaten ground floor. There was nothing ornamental, and no superfluous furniture. A bedstead standing in one corner, with some pieces of white tappa cloth of the island for curtains, whereon was laid a pile of mats for a bed; two or three piles of mats laying along near the centre of the hut, raised one or two feet from the floor, by being piled one above the other, for beds or lounging places; two or three old chairs; a plain table of small dimensions, and a dressing-case with a mirror in it, was all of Boque's furniture, either useful or ornamental. Besides these may be mentioned a few hollow gourds for poye, (a favourite food of the Sandwich Islanders, made from the tarrow,) hanging at the side of the hut.

Leaving Boque's palace, we went with the intention of making a similar call upon the high chief Crimacu, known to strangers who have visited the island, by the name of Billy Pitt. He was the high carnie, or great friend of Tamahamaha, in whose wars he was greatly distinguished for personal prowess, sagacity, and wisdom. When we came to his hut, we found him sleeping in a swinging cot, with several attendants sitting round, one of whom was fanning him. He was in very ill health, having for a long time been afflicted with the dropsy, and we departed without waking him. His hut differed in nothing from that of Boque, except that it was not so large, and had a greater profusion of mats in it. It was standing in one corner of an extensive plain, that was partially enclosed by a wicker fence just at the outskirts of the town of Onaroora, and all around it was growing wild grass and weeds, except where the footsteps of the people, who passed to and from the hut, had trodden them down. It looked but little like the habitation of a man who had been a great warrior, and associated as second in authority with one who had conquered and ruled over thousands of men. One would naturally suppose that in emerging from a savage state, with absolute power, he would have made an attempt, at least, to imitate the style and manners of the white men with whom he was constantly meeting, and always on terms of friendship.

After we had interchanged salutes with the shore, chief Boque came on board on the 17th, to make us a visit of ceremony. He was dressed in a splendid English major-general's uniform, and made a very handsome appearance. He remained and partook of a collation with us, at which several gentlemen were invited to meet him, and in all respects acquitted himself in a more polite and becoming manner than could have been expected from one whose opportunities had been so limited. He drank sparingly of wine, and left us at an early hour, notwithstanding the solicitations of the company for him to remain. A few hours after he had landed, I met him again, and should hardly have recognized him but for his large stature and good-natured face. He had stripped himself of all his finery, and was walking over the plain from his house with nothing on but his marrow, and a piece of tappa cloth of the island thrown loosely over his shoulders. I asked him why he had taken off his uniform, to which he replied, that it was too warm.

Our countrymen, to vary the entertainments they were constantly giving us, and thereby make

P

them the more acceptable, proposed that we should make an excursion to a valley, called by them Pearl River, from the pearl frequently found in a small stream that passes through it. As horses could not be obtained for all, part of the company went by water, whilst the rest, four or five, mounted on horseback. The distance was about fifteen miles. I made one of the land party, and we set off early in the afternoon. There was no road, and in many places not even a footpath. The whole way was over hill and dale, and through swamps. We had to jump fences and ditches made through tarrow-patches, and ascend by narrow paths, difficult and dangerous cliffs. All the afternoon was occupied in this manner, and it was sundown when we arrived at our place of destination. One old native made bold to oppose us in jumping our horses over his fence, and was so obstinate in his refusal to let us pass, that for a time we thought we should have to relinquish our excursion—a reflection not very agreeable, after having advanced more than half way over so wretched a road. Finally, when all other arguments had failed, some one of the party, thinking that the native opposed our trespass upon his premises with no other object than to lay us under contribution, gave him half a dollar, which did more for us than all our threats or persuasion. Instead of opposing, he afterwards pointed

out to us the best way. From Onavoora to Pearl
River, the country was thinly inhabited. We
met with no considerable village or rich valley.
Our road lay near the edge of a wide marsh, that
intervened between us and the sea, in the opposite
direction from which, an undulating country extended three or four miles, when it was interrupted by the high and uninhabited range of
mountains that run through the centre of the
island from one end to the other. It was Saturday evening, when we arrived at Pearl River,
and, according to the doctrine in which the missionaries had instructed the Sandwich islanders,
their sabbath had commenced. The hut that we
were to occupy belonged to Captain Dana, an
American gentleman, to whom we were indebted
for many hours of agreeable pastime. Besides
the hut, he possessed other property in the valley,
which gave him an influence with the chief of it,
that enabled him to command whatever it produced. When we arrived, the chief was seated
on a mat, near Captain Danas' hut, moody, and,
apparently, very stupid. The arrival of so many
strangers, in a place where a visiter was scarcely
ever seen, produced a lively interest amongst the
villagers. All of them seemed to partake of the
general excitement, but the chief, though celebrated for his hospitality, was now sunk in the
most listless apathy, and apparently scarcely sen-

sible of our presence. When he was told that we wanted supper, and preparation made for our accommodation on the morrow, he replied, that it was the sabbath, and neither then nor on the morrow could fire be made, as it was forbidden by the Almighty. Upon being asked how he knew that it was forbidden by the Almighty, he said, that Mr. Bingham had seen the Almighty, who told him so. This was a great check to our promised enjoyment, and one that we were quite unprepared for, as no prohibition of making fire on Saturday, or any other night, was in existence at Onavoora. We saw but a poor prospect of getting supper or any thing, indeed, until we returned, unless we fasted on Sunday, and that our religious scruples did not call for, if it were not unavoidable. We were unwilling, however, to interfere with the established observances, which had been thought necessary to civilize and improve the condition of the people, and bore our disappointment in silence. After wandering about the village for a while, which was small, and scattered over a sterile ridge, we were relieved from our unpleasant dilemma by a native, we had taken with us as cook and interpreter, who was commonly known upon the island by the name of Joe Banks. He had received some education, and had been a convert to the missionaries, from whom he afterwards seceded. He did not like fasting any more than ourselves, and set about haranguing the chief, to convince him of the error of his opinion, with respect to the making of fire. Joe was not wanting in either talent or volubility; and, to our great satisfaction, we soon found him on good terms with the chief; a fire was made, and soon after a kid and a pig brought up for slaughter. I observed, that the chief's skin was very rough and in scales, resembling somewhat the shell of a small terrapin. Upon inquiring the cause, they told me, it was the effect of the ava-root, of which he was undergoing a course. He had almost finished the course, and his skin was all peeling off. It was the effect of the ava, that made him so stupid, and under its operation he was a most disgusting looking object. The natives of the Sandwich Islands are very much subject to cutaneous irruptions, which are troublesome, and, when of long standing, often dangerous. To eradicate this, and some other offensive diseases, with which they are afflicted, they sometimes go through a course of the ava. It is taken in quantities from a gill to half a pint, of the juice of the green root. It is chewed, and the juice spit into a gourd, if intended for the use of another person than the one who prepares it, and is said, when taken, to deprive the person of muscular power. In a few moments after swallowing the potion, he loses the use of all his limbs. He experiences an agreeable sensation, and is conscious of every thing that transpires, but without the power of speech. He lies in this helpless condition for several hours, when he recovers his strength in a measure, and is left in the condition of a man that has been very much intoxicated. This, to have the desired effect, is repeated daily for about a month; when the disease is cured, the skin all comes off, and a fair and shining one is left in its place. When once it was settled between Joe Banks and the chief of Pearl River Valley, that fire should be made, and our supper cooked, he provided for us in the most sumptuous native style. We had pigs, goats, fish, tarrow, and potatoes, in the greatest profusion. All was cooked after the manner of the natives, and as the same method is practised generally amongst the islanders of the Pacific Ocean, and knowing, from experience, that it is a very good one, I will here describe it. A hole is first dug a foot or two deep, and large, according to the size of the thing to be cooked. A fire is then made in the hole, and, when it is burning well, covered over with stones of a convenient size. When every thing is in readiness, the stones being well heated, they are taken off, and the hole cleared out. A layer of stones is then placed all round the interior, upon which is lain the meat, after being well wrapped up in green leaves. Over this is placed a thick layer of stones, which is covered with grass, or something dry, and then with earth. If vegetables are to be cooked, they are lain on the top of the upper layer of stones. The young tops of the tarrow are usually wrapped up in leaves, and cooked with the meats in the manner above described. It is a very excellent green, and called by the natives lewoca, from which the method of cooking takes its name. Early in the morning after our arrival, we arose, to look upon the wild beauty of the valley, and wander through what, at a distance, appeared to be its meadows and lawns ; but, to our great disappointment, in descending from the hills, the green level fields that looked so pleasant at a distance, were all cut up in tarrow patches, flooded over, and intersected in every direction with ditches and embankments. A scene, so uninviting, soon induced us to relinquish our anticipated pleasure, and return.

In the course of our morning's walk we came to the house of an Englishman, who, a few years previous, arrived at the island in a Peruvian man-of-war, the seamen of which had risen upon their officers, and ran away with the vessel. He had taken to himself a native wife, and, to all appearance, had fixed here his abode for life. His hut looked extremely comfortable—not less so, indeed, than that of the chief, and besides other property that he had acquired, he had a fine flock of sheep feeding near his residence. He politely invited us into his house, which we declined, as we were returning late to breakfast.

After breakfast we set off in our boat to visit a small island near the sea shore, where there were a great many rabbits. We passed along several miles of an inlet of the sea, before we came to it. It was half a mile long, level, and overgrown with high weeds. The rabbits were so numerous, that the island was every where perforated with their burrows, and one or more would be found in almost every bunch of high grass that we came to,—so tame, that we could frequently take them up in our hands. We caught more than a dozen of them in this way, in the short time that we remained. Some years previous, an old Spaniard, by the name of Menini, who had settled at Onavoora, put one or more pairs of rabbits upon this small island, and prevailed upon the chiefs to tabboo them. From that time they had not been disturbed.

After returning to our dinner, we all set off on our way back to Onavoora. To vary the scene, I relinquished my horse and took passage in the boat. We sailed for several miles among marshes and barren islands, upon a salt water inlet, up which a ship of heavy burthen might pass for a considerable distance. The whole way was quite void of interest. When we got to the sea, we had a head wind to row against all the way. A reef extended out from the shore, beyond which we were compelled to go, making the distance so great, that the evening was far advanced before we got to the Dolphin.

Not long after our return from Pearl River, I set out one day with an American gentleman, to ascend a high and steep mountain, that rises back of the village, which the natives, many years ago, fortified with a few heavy pieces of cannon. We crossed the plain, which is a mile or a mile and a half wide, when we came to the base of the mountain. It was seven or eight hundred feet high, and from below, seemed to rise almost perpendicular from the plain. A winding footpath, however, showed us that it had long and frequently been ascended by the natives, and encouraged us to make the attempt. We had often to stop and get breath, but at last accomplished our object, by gaining the summit and entering upon a small plain. Here we found several huts, that were occupied by the families of the men appointed to guard this important post, into which we entered to obtain leave to examine the fortification. The people were very friendly ; they not only granted us permission, but hospitably proffered us some excellent melons, which were very refreshing after our laborious ascent. There were only three men in the fort, one of whom, that appeared to have the command, politely waited upon us in our walk round. The guns were mounted on a platform, at the very edge of the precipice that overlooked the harbour and town. They were of thirty-two pound caliber. It must have been a work of inconceivable labour for the natives to get them upon this great eminence. The carriages and all their fixtures were very much decayed, and totally unfit for use. The situation is very commanding, and notwithstanding the distance, the battery would be formidable to an enemy in the harbour. From this eminence, we had an extensive and beautiful prospect, comprehending the valley and harbour, many miles at sea, and along the sea-coast in either direction. The river, that waters the valley, broken in cataracts as it rapidly descended to the sea, showed to its greatest advantage, and the valley, covered with its tarrow patches, corn, and potatoes, presented a landscape resembling finely cultivated fields and waving green meadows. In front, was the thatched village of Onavoora, the huts looking like heaps of dry straw; beyond it, the harbour and shipping; and still farther, at sea, a long range of white foaming breakers. On the extreme right, was the valley of Pearl River, bounded by high and rugged mountains; and to the left, the cocoa-nut groves

of Whytete and Diamond Rock, with its adjacent
sterile hills, covered with volcanic cinders.

From the top of the hill, we descended in a different direction on our return, with a view of
passing through a part of the valley that runs far
back from the shore between the mountains,
where it appeared to be finely cultivated and well
inhabited. We had not gone far from the fort,
when we found ourselves near the centre of what
had been the crater of a volcano, and which, from
its resemblance, has given the eminence the name
of the Punch Bowl, by which it is familiarly
known amongst foreigners. The crater is about
a quarter or half a mile in diameter, and from one
to two hundred feet deep. When we descended
to the valley, which was not without difficulty,
our way was every where interrupted by tarrow
patches, their ditches, and embankments. After
crossing a small valley, we came to an elevated
piece of ground, where the natives who cultivated
the tarrow below, had built their habitations, and
around them planted groves of Banana. It was a
fine morning, and the people of both sexes were
industriously engaged in their appropriate occu-
pations. Some of the women were roasting tarrow, and others making it up in poye. The latter
operation was interesting to me, as I had never
seen it before. When the tarrow is roasted, and
the skin taken off, it resembles a potatoe ; it is

then put into a tray, and with a long, smooth stone, beaten up as fine as possible, occasionally mixing a small quantity of water with it; after it has been beaten in this way, it is worked over a number of times, to get all the lumps out; it then has the appearance of a thick paste or starch. As soon as it foments a little and becomes slightly acid, it is used. When in this state, it will not last long before it becomes very sour, and is then considered so unwholesome, that unless the people are very poor, it is thrown away.

After satisfying our curiosity in seeing the women make poye, we descended the hill where several men were preparing a tarrow patch. It was forty feet square, excavated a little, and an embankment two feet high thrown up all around it, descending with a considerable angle from the top to the base, making it very broad at the bottom. The labourers had advanced thus far, and were beating the area and inner sides of the embankment with broad heavy paddles, going over it a great many times. It appeared very hard and firm when we saw them at work; but still, they told us, that they had to beat it a great deal more. When this is completed, the tops of the tarrow that have been cut off for the purpose, are set in the ground and lightly flooded with water; after it has taken root and began to grow thriftily, more water is let in upon it; the tarrow well grown, will generally be covered with water to the depth of one or two feet. It is about the size of a beet, and takes a year or more to come to its greatest perfection. It has clusters of broad bright green leaves, that in shape and appearance are a good deal like the common pond lilly. It is a very nutricious vegetable, and constitutes the principal means of subsistence of the Sandwich Islanders.

The huts of the natives were very small, and although in the midst of cultivation and fertility, the inhabitants seemed to be wretchedly poor. They did not appear much more civilized than the natives of the Marquesas; their habitations were certainly less comfortable. Returning to the village, we saw a number of people scraping sticks that looked like our elder, and preserving the inner bark. Upon inquiring its use, they told us it was to catch fish with. When eaten by the fish, they come to the top of the water and are taken out by hand. It is said, the fish are not the worse for this.

On our arrival at Oahoo, the Dolphin was out of repair in every respect, and it was indispensably necessary to refit her, before we proceeded further on our return to the coast of Chili or Peru. Whilst the masts were out, and the vessel was undergoing general repairs, the captain received a letter from Captain Edwards, of the ship Loudon, of New-York, stating that he had ran upon a reef, on the Island of Ranai; besides a valuable cargo, he had a large amount of specie and bullion on board. The chief Thunder, (chief of Ranai,) was encouraging the natives of the island to plunder him, and finally, that his life and treasure was in the greatest jeopardy. Although not incumbent upon him as a duty, Captain Percival, with a promptitude highly creditable to himself and the service to which he belonged, chartered a vessel, and with the crew of the Dolphin, and Boque, the Governor of Oahoo, sailed on the same day that he received the letter. He found the situation of Captain Edwards not less critical than he had described it to be. The natives had already plundered him of a part of his cargo, and his own crew was in a state of mutiny. Employing the authority of Chief Boque, and the indefatigable industry of his own crew, Captain Percival caused the stolen goods to be restored, and the cargo and treasure of the Loudon to be safely landed at Oahoo. When all this had been accomplished, Captain Edwards refused to pay the charter of the vessel that was employed for his relief, in consequence of which, a quarrel arose between himself and Captain Percival, that eventuated in consequences injurious and disagreeable to both parties, and after our return home, became a subject of judicial investigation. By this investigation, which was brought on at the instance of Captain Edwards, an opportunity was afforded to Captain Percival and the officers of the Dolphin, to vindicate their characters, which they did, in every instance, to the entire satisfaction of their government and countrymen.

Whilst Captain Percival was absent at Ranai, Captain Jackson, of the brig Harbinger, of Boston, addressed a letter to me, stating that his store in the village had been broken open, and robbed of goods to a large amount, and requesting my assistance to recover them. The matter was laid before the chief, Crimacu, who instituted a search, and on the following day, sent for Captain Jackson. At his hut, were assembled most of the foreigners of any respectability on the island, and many of the natives to witness the result of the inquiry. Some of the thieves had already been detected, and now stood before the chief, who, although very ill, sat up to question them about the robbery. They confessed their guilt, and in answering the questions put to them, convicted others, who were sent for and brought in, until the number amounted to six. They had shared their booty, and were sent out, with guards, to bring it from their different places of concealment. It consisted, principally, of fine calicoes and cloths, which had been put in tarrow patches, and oil casks, and when returned, were so damaged, as to be of but little value to the owner. When the chief got through with the inquiry, and had collected all the goods that could be found, he asked Mr. Jackson what punishment he would have inflicted upon the offenders. Mr. Jackson's reply was, that he wanted restitution made for the loss he had sustained, and that he would leave the punishment to the chief, according to the usage of the islands. The chief contended that the men were all poor, and had nothing wherewith to pay. He said that the chiefs were also poor, and denied the justice of compelling them, under any circumstances, to pay for the thefts of the people. He offered to put the culprits at Captain Jackson's disposal, or inflict upon them whatever punishment he should prescribe, according to the laws of his own country. Captain Jackson refused to say what punishment the men should receive, and only contended that the chief was bound to see his property, or an equivalent, restored to him. The matter was, for some hours in debate, when the chief compromised with Captain Jackson, by promising to have a quantity of sandal-wood collected for him within a prescribed period. The thieves were set at liberty without punishment, in consequence of which, it was surmised by some of our countrymen, that the chiefs had been concerned in the theft. This, I thought, a very unjust suspicion, as the investigation took place so publicly, that the fact, if it had been so, could hardly have failed to appear in the course of the inquiry.

The magnanimity of Crimacu,* in promising an equivalent for the damaged goods, which he was not bound to do by the customs of the Sandwich Islands, or the laws of civilized communities, gave me the highest opinion of his character. It appeared to me that he first objected to remunerate the merchant for his loss, with no other motive than to produce discussion, from which he might learn what would be done in more enlightened countries, in a similar case. He was told of the different punishments that the culprits would be subject to under the laws of America and England, but nothing could be advanced, even supposing that he was to act in accordance with the laws of those countries, to prove that the chiefs or king of the islands, were in any other way responsible for the thefts committed by individuals, than to make them stand forth and suffer in person for their offences. He remarked, that the information he received from individuals of the same country, with respect to their laws and customs, was often at variance, and so contradictory, that he was frequently at a loss to know what he should do to answer the ends of justice, and give satisfaction to the strangers who came to the

---

* Crimacu, as it is pronounced by the natives. The missionaries write his name Karaimoku.

Q

islands. He declared, that the chiefs of the Sandwich Islands, wished to do like other people.

Amongst those with whom we held frequent and friendly intercourse, was an Englishman, by the name of Wilkinson, who had taken passage to the Sandwich Islands, in the Frigate Blonde, when she went there with the remains of king Rio Rio, and who had banished himself from his own country to this distant region, with a view of becoming a planter of the Sandwich Islands. He had been, according to his own statement, a planter in the West Indies in early life, and subsequently on his return to England, joined a troop of horse, of which he was a captain, destined for Spain, during the war in the Peninsula, where he served for a considerable time, but at the close of the war, having left the army, and met with a reverse of fortune, he had determined to make the experiment in which he was now engaged. A bold one, it must be confessed, for a man, at the age of forty-five, and with an enfeebled constitution. Aided by Captain Byron, (who, from his high rank, and the flattering mission upon which he had been sent, was well prepared to assist him,) Mr. Wilkinson obtained from the chiefs the first deed that ever was granted by them, for two hundred acres of land. It was situated about six miles from Onavoora, on elevated ground, bordering upon a narrow valley that winds through the

mountains for several miles back from the sea.
The chiefs granted the deed with great reluctance, notwithstanding the respectable source
from which the petition came, being extremely
tenacious of that command and sovereignty of the
soil, that enables them, at pleasure, to dispossess
the occupant. They the more willingly relinquished the spot that Mr. Wilkinson had fixed
upon for his residence, as it was situated upon
land so high, that it could not be used for the
culture of tarrow, and was at the time unoccupied. With uncommon industry, although cramp-
ed by the want of money, that would have given
it its full effect, he had reclaimed from a wild
state, about fifty acres of land, which, when we
arrived there, was planted with sugar-cane, corn,
potatoes, bananas, &c., thus providing for his immediate wants, whilst the cane promised a rich
harvest, that would amply reward him for his toil,
whenever he could complete his machinery for
the manufacture of sugar. In this, however, to
all appearance when we were there, he would encounter great difficulty, as materials were not
easily obtained; and although there were some
mechanics on the island, their constant employment in the village, where they could frequently
see their countrymen, and withal, their fondness
for pleasure was likely to deprive him for a long
time of their useful services, without which, he

could do nothing. Connected with his land, was a stream of water running from the mountains, that would answer his purpose for manufacturing sugar. In a part of it that possessed all local advantages, he had made a dam and collected part of the materials for a mill, to be constructed in the simplest manner, but which, for the want of mechanical aid, lay in almost the same rude state in which he had purchased them. He anticipated, however, with great confidence, that by the time the cane was ready for cutting, the mill would be prepared, when the hopes by which he had first been stimulated, could scarcely fail to be realized. The sugar cane grows wild upon the Sandwich Islands, and Mr. Wilkinson's fields were from the native growth, which he had planted in prepared land, and at our departure, the canes were upwards of six feet high.

Although several strangers, familiar with the arts of civilized countries, have settled and lived, for many years, amongst the Sandwich Islanders, Mr. Wilkinson was the first individual who ever attempted to put them in practice, upon a scale, sufficiently extensive to improve, materially, the agricultural condition of the islands, and thereby prove to the inhabitants the wealth they possess, in a rich soil, and one of the finest climates on the face of the globe. Should Mr. Wilkinson be successful, the result of his experiment will probably do more towards the civilization of the natives, and their ultimate advancement in knowledge and lasting prosperity, than has yet been effected by all the white men that have lived amongst them. This, I am aware, will be considered a rash assertion by the good people of our country, who, from the best of motives, feel deeply engaged in foreign missions; and, in expressing this opinion, I will also bear testimony to the useful services of the missionaries. From the best information that I could obtain upon the subject, I am satisfied, that they have improved the morals of the people, and if they devote themselves to the schools that they have established, and to introducing the arts of life and civilization, the time may not be distant, when the natives will be prepared to receive Christianity. But in their present condition, would it not be better, and more in the true spirit of that benevolence and philanthropy which is inspired by our religion, to teach them how to cultivate their land, to introduce grain and fruits, congenial to the climate, and to plant and reap as we do, rather than imbue their minds with a mysterious doctrine, which, being beyond their comprehension, must resolve itself into a dark and intolerant superstition.

The inhabitants of the Sandwich Islands, are mild, amiable, and intelligent, and susceptible of the highest degree of moral and intellectual improvement.   As a people, it may be said, that the stamp of civilization is scarcely perceptible yet upon them; and it is now inevitable, that they must bear the impress of those, whom our philanthropists have sent to convert them to Christianity; and, whether they become ignorant zealots, or intelligent Christians, will depend upon their teachers.   The situation of these missionaries is, therefore, one of high responsibility, and ought not, in Christian charity, to be occupied by the narrow-minded fanatic, or the ignorant zealot. It is of the first importance that they, who dispose of the vast means of the missionary society, should select only such men for civilizing and Christianizing the Sandwich Islanders, as are distinguished for their knowledge, and love of the useful arts of life, as well as for practical piety.

The harbour of Onavoora, is a place of general rendezvous for the whale ships, cruising on the coast of Japan, and in the vicinity of the islands.   The months of January, February, and March, being the least favourable for their business, they then leave their cruising ground, and go in search of refreshment.   No place is so convenient for them as the Sandwich Islands, and the port of Onavoora, being the most commodious of any in the group, and affording an abundant supply of vegetables, hogs, &c.,—they all congregate there in the months above mentioned.

The average number that visit the island in the course of the year, is upwards of fifty. More than twenty were there together, at several different periods of our stay, some of which remained a few days, some weeks, and a few one or two months, according to their several necessities. At such times the seamen, from having been long confined to the narrow precinct of their vessels, become very insubordinate, and frequently give way to the most licentious indulgences of their passions, regardless of every obligation of obedience due to their officers. We witnessed frequent instances of this kind, and had the satisfaction of being constantly useful to the captains of ships, and the whaling interest, by restraining the violent, and coercing them to a proper sense of duty.

A most unpleasant occurrence took place about six weeks after our arrival at Onavoora, arising from this disposition of the seamen, and other causes, which was afterwards greatly misrepresented in this country. Some of the seamen of the Dolphin, who were on liberty, got into a frolic, and, associating themselves with many others belonging to the whale ships, determined to go to the houses of the high chiefs and missionaries, and demand the repeal of a restriction that deprived them of the society of females. They produced a riot that gave rise to a consid-

erable degree of excitement for a few minutes;
but Captain Percival, with some of the officers of
the Dolphin, and captains of whale-ships, promptly suppressed it, and prevented any serious outrage. It was afterwards unjustly and most un-
generously ascribed to the officers of the Dolphin.

The white population of Onavoora is of a varied
character, from the agent of our North West
traders, to the most abandoned members of society. There are from fifty to a hundred, permanently settled at Onavoora; the least respectable of whom, maintain themselves by keeping
tippling shops for sailors, and practising such
chicaneries as are suggested by opportunities and
the absence of law. The season for the whalers
to visit the Island is the time of their harvest,
when, besides their gains from entertaining the
seamen, they frequently prevail upon them to de-
sert for the sake of the reward for their apprehension, or to strip them of what little money or
clothes they may be possessed of. Some of them
have married women of the Island, and live much
in the same way as the natives. Of all the per-
manent settlers at Onavoora, the most remarkable was a Spaniard by the name of Meninne, who
had been in the Islands upwards of thirty years.
Of his manner of getting there, a variety of sto-
ries were told. His own account was, that being
invited on board of a vessel that visited the coast

of California, he fell asleep in the evening, and, when he awoke, found himself at sea, and the vessel running, with a fair wind, for the Sandwich Islands. All his entreaties to be returned to land were in vain, and he arrived at Owhyhee, where, poor and friendless, he was landed amongst the natives. He wandered from island to island, in a forlorn and wretched condition, until he was taken under the patronage of Tamahamaha. For a long time, he followed the fortunes of the native warrior, and at length fixed his residence at Oahoo, from whence he occasionally embarked as interpreter on board of merchant vessels, bound on smuggling voyages to the coast of America. After passing through a variety of fortune, being several times made prisoner and threatened with death, he finally quitted his vagrant life, and remained permanently at Oahoo, where, by great industry and economy, he has acquired an amount of property which, for that place, is a princely fortune. Besides having money in the United States and England, he owns nearly all the cattle on the Island of Oahoo, a number of horses, flocks of goats, sheep, &c. He has extensive possessions in land, which he holds from the chiefs in consideration of his services, and a great many houses. He has taken some pains to introduce exotics in the Islands, and besides the lemon, orange, and other valuable fruits, has a vineyard from which he makes a considerable quantity of wine annually. He is said to be extremely selfish, and so jealous of preserving to himself a monopoly of these valuable fruits, that he has been accused of destroying the young plants of others. He is considered as ranking amongst the chiefs in the enjoyment of certain privileges; and, speaking the language of the Islands well, is called upon as interpreter for the government upon all important occasions. He has had thirty-seven children by various wives, and is yet in the prime of life. Like most men who have felt the cold hand of poverty, and afterwards acquired wealth, he is extremely penurious, and thinks of nothing so much as adding to his fortune without knowing how to enjoy it.

On the 3d of April, the young king and all the high chiefs, were invited on board to spend the day with us. In the morning, we dressed the schooner in all the flags we could muster, and made the best preparation our limited accommodation would admit of to receive our distinguished guests. No indication of their appearance was seen for some time after every thing was in readiness, and our boats on shore in waiting, and we were kept in suspense until we had almost despaired of seeing them. All at once the whole town was in an uproar, and the people were running and hallooing in every direction. The young

king in advance, walked arm in arm with one of
the officers of the Dolphin. Next came Boque
and his spouse, with other high dignitaries, and
in the rear a multitude of people of both sexes
and all ages. When they had embarked, the
eyes of the people were turned upon another object, not less interesting to them than the king.
Crimacu, or Billy Pitt, too ill to walk, was grave-
ly making his way to the beach in a hand cart,
where he got into a boat and came on board soon
after the king. We received them with manned
yards, and a salute of twenty-one guns. The
king, who was a boy of ten or twelve years old,
was dressed in a military uniform that was sent
to him from the king of England, and upon his
shoulders he wore a pair of golden epaulets, with
crowns on them. He appeared to be sensible of
his rank, and, upon two or three occasions, addressed his attendants in a way that indicated a
wish to make a display of his authority. The
chiefs conducted themselves towards him with a
becoming respect, but without bestowing upon
him any attention that might interfere with their
own enjoyment or convenience. Instead of par-
taking of what we had provided for our guests,
they, with one or two exceptions, unceremoniously uncovered their poye pots, which had been
brought with them by an attendant, and ate heartily of their favourite food, using their fingers as is

the native custom. Boque again displayed his major general's uniform, and was amongst the most polished of our guests. After passing a number of hours on board, they returned to the shore delighted with their visit. The same compliment was paid them as at their reception. It was a day of great enjoyment with the common people. They received their chiefs on landing with loud huzzas, and followed them in crowds to their respective habitations.

We passed all the winter months at Onavoora, during which we had frequent heavy rains. Some of the storms were attended with violent gales, and disagreeably cold weather. About the 3d of May, an influenza made its appearance amongst the inhabitants of Oahoo, and in two days not a well native was any where to be seen. The market, from being well attended, was deserted. In a week, the distress was so general and so great, that it was feared the poor people would perish with hunger. I visited several families, not a member of which was able to help himself or others, and all were totally destitute of food. A great many of the people died, and amongst the rest two chiefs, one of whom was George Tamauri, a native of the Island of Atooi, who was educated in this country. The other was Cahaliha, next in affinity to the king. Scarcely any of the white people were affected. Not even those living on shore. In about ten days, the people from the country began to make their appearance in the market, the distress was greatly alleviated, and soon afterwards the general good health restored. At such times of suffering, the condition of these people is truly wretched. They have no floor to their huts but the hard-beaten ground from which their naked bodies are separated only by two or three thin mats, and during the rainy season the earth becomes perfectly saturated with water. Their huts are generally built in a very frail manner, and in a driving storm are not proof against the rain. This, alone, is sufficient to account for the thinly populated state of the islands, without charging the natives with the acts of inhumanity that have been ascribed to them by some people.

The harbour of Onavoora is formed by coral reefs, that extend upwards of a mile from the shore. The entrance to it is narrow and somewhat difficult. It affords water enough for a sloop of war. A pilot in and out of the harbour, is always employed. It is very secure, being quite land locked. The holding ground is good, and vessels may lay in safety close along side of the beach. The water is perfectly smooth in good weather, and the bottom and shores being nearly every where of soft mud, a vessel might be driven upon them in a gale without sustaining any material injury. The visits of the numerous whale ships has made Onavoora a place of considerable trade. All of them spend more or less money for their necessary refreshments, and when out of repair, their disbursements are frequently very considerable. For the supplies afforded by the natives, thousands of dollars are annually received by them, which they give in return for silk, cotton, calicoes, cloth, &c. Two or three stores, well stocked with a great variety of goods, are supported in Onavoora by this interchange of commodities; and, from the way in which the trade is conducted, there is but little doubt that the proprietors are rewarded with handsome profits. The sandal wood has become scarce upon the islands, from the large quantities formerly taken away by our traders, and does not now form a very lucrative or extensive article of commerce. Upon this article, some of our merchants are said to have made large sums of money in exchange for whole cargoes of goods, with the chiefs of the Sandwich Islands. It is related of Tamahamaha, that, after making a purchase of this kind, which he paid for in ship loads of sandal wood, brought from the mountains with great labour to himself and people, he has been known to load a number of canoes secretly at night, with fine broadcloths, and take them out to sea, where he sunk them with stones. His only reason for it was, that the possession of them would make his chiefs and people too luxurious and idle, and bringing sandal wood from the mountains to pay for more, would give them employment. A doubtful policy, certainly, if the statement be true. Be this as it may, himself and successor have entailed upon their descendants a national debt of several hundred thousands of dollars, now due to our merchants, which they will not soon be able to liquidate.

On the 11th of May, after long anticipating our much wished for departure, we got underway, and saluting the fort as we passed it with twenty-one guns, stood out to sea and shaped our course for Chili. Nothing material transpired from the time of our sailing until the 7th of June, when standing along with a fresh trade, and the night dark and squally, at 10 P. M., the lookout-ahead reported land close aboard. We tacked and lay to for the night, to survey our newly discovered island on the following morning. At daylight, it bore S. S. W., about six miles from us, and appeared in three small hummocs, covered thickly with trees and bushes, every where bounded by a coral reef and heavy surf. We hesitated for some time whether we should land, apprehending that it would be attended with too much risk, merely for the gratification of curiosity; but this feeling operated so powerfully upon us, that there

was no resisting the desire to land where no one
had ever been before. Accordingly, two boats
were sent off, and watching a favourable opportunity passed through the surf in safety, and
landed on the coral bank where they were left
high and dry by the receding wave. It was on
the lee side of the island, and a coral reef stretched off about fifty or a hundred yards from the
shore, full of holes, and almost dry at low water.
In the holes we sought for fish, as at Caroline
Island, but found very few. On traversing the
island, we could find no fruit or vegetable of any
description except bup. In most places it was
covered with trees and bushes of a thick growth,
almost impenetrable. In the bushes we found a
great many tropical birds setting, so tame that
we could take them off of their nests with our
hands, and in getting upon the weather side of
the island where there was a clear space, we
found a species of small gull, so numerous, that
when they rose from the ground at our approach,
they appeared to form almost a compact mass.
The sand was literally covered with their eggs,
which, upon examination, proved to be unfit for
use, with few exceptions. The birds flew and
hovered so near to us that we caught several of
them with our hands. After amusing ourselves
a little while with the novel spectacle of such
numbers of birds so very tame, we collected all

the old eggs within a small space, and in less than twenty minutes after it had been thus cleared, it was again covered with fresh eggs by the birds that were constantly lighting. We might, in a few hours, have loaded our boats with them. When we returned to our boats to go on board, the tide had risen, and with it the surf had increased to an alarming degree. At first, we held a consultation whether we should attempt to pass through it or remain until it should again subside with the falling of the tide; but the day was far advanced, and the appearance of the weather such, as in all probability would render our situation extremely painful, there being every prospect of an increase of wind. We therefore determined to put our fortune to the test, and were not a little discouraged when on one of the boats attempting the surf was thrown back by the second roller that she encountered with the utmost violence, upsetting her, and scattering the people in different directions, some of them escaping with their lives with the greatest difficulty. Notwithstanding the ill success of our first attempt, we determined on a second, rather than risk the consequences of longer delay. Embracing a favourable opportunity where the surf appeared least violent, we put off, and passed through it in safety without further accident.

R

The island was little more than a mile long, and from a hundred yards to a quarter of a mile wide. It was every where very low. By a meridian observation, we placed the north-west end of it in latitude south 21 degrees 48 minutes, and longitude by chronometer 154 degrees 54 minutes west. In compliment to the commander of our squadron in the Pacific Ocean, we called it Hull's Island. It may be comprehended within the group of Society Islands.

In the afternoon, June the 4th, we made sail; and on the following day at half-past 6 o'clock, A.M. discovered the island of Ramitaria, on the lee bow, about eight leagues from us. This island was not laid down in any of our charts, having been discovered only three or four years before; but we had seen a gentlemen who had stopped there, and it was included in our list of islands. On approaching it we were pleased to find that it differed from many of the islands we had visited, being of a moderate elevation. It is about three miles long and one or two wide. We ran nearly round it before we found a place to land, the surf breaking high every where, and the shores bounded by large rocks of coral. At last, we came to the principal settlement, which was situated close to the shore, where a large white-washed house indicated the former visits and influences of the missionaries. The people, to the number of one or two hundred, were assembled on the beach inviting us to land. Here, also, was a considerable surf and some coral rocks, which made the landing not altogether free from difficulty. When the boat came near the shore and while she was yet shooting rapidly through the surf, the natives, who had already advanced to meet us, laid hold as many as could get round her, and with loud shouting, carried us high upon the beach. At this somewhat unexpected reception, the boats' crew instinctively seized their pistols, thinking at first, that the natives were hostile in their disposition towards us. It was but a momentery panic which passed away with the kind salutations we immediately afterwards received. When I enquired for the chief, a young man was pointed out to me in the crowd, distinguished from the rest by an old hat on his head, that he had obtained from some former visiter. He seemed not to be treated with the least respect by the people, who jostled him in the crowd with the most perfect carelessness. Scarcely had I addressed him, when a stout native came up with an air of some importance, and saluting me, told me in the language of the Society Islands, that he was the missionary. Upon his approach, the chief immediately shrunk back into the crowd. He called to him a Malay, who was not far off, and bade him ask what we wanted. The Malay, whose name was Manoo, spoke English very well, which was a source of great satisfaction to us, as we could thereby communicate our wants freely, and it introduced us at once to each others' acquaintance. I explained to Manoo that we were in want of water and such refreshments as the island might afford. He immediately proceeded in company with the missionary to show me where water was to be obtained. We passed through a forest of very large trees over a plain that extended more than half a mile, when we came to a marsh of reeds and rank grass, where there was from one to two feet of water, covering an area of two or three acres. This would not answer our purpose as the water was not very good, and its distance from the place of embarkation rendered it too laborious an undertaking to water the vessel from it. When I had remarked this to Manoo and the missionary, they replied that there was better water, but it was still more distant. I suffered them to conduct me to it, and we took a footpath over rising ground, and through another delightful forest of bread-fruit and other wide-spreading trees, passing many fine tarrow patches, and at the distance of half a mile from the marsh, we came to a spring of excellent water. Manoo and the missionary both expressed a great deal of disappointment when I spoke in

terms of disapprobation of this also as a watering-
place—it being altogether too far from the shore.

On our return from the spring, we took a different footpath from that by which we came, and
ascended to a more elevated part of the island to
see the work of the missionary, as it was called
by Manoo. This consisted of two or three enclosures by means of stakes, in the midst of the
forest, where the trees had been cut down for
several acres, which was cleared and planted
with sweet potatoes and tobacco. The enclosures
were made, and all the labour of clearing the
forest was done, as Manoo remarked, by such of
the wicked and disobedient, as had resisted the
authority and ordinances of the white missionary
during his residence on the island some months
previous. Since then, the white missionary had
returned to Otaheite, and sent this native missionary, who belonged to that island, to represent
him in his absence. Leaving the enclosures of
tobacco and sweet potatoes, we came into a thicket where the trees were overrun with the vines of
the yam, growing wild and covered with beautiful blue flowers that gave a picturesque appearance to the forest, and filled it with their fra-
grance. We passed five or six stone columns
that had been sixty or seventy feet high, and
twenty or thirty in circumference. They were
in a dilapidated state, having in part been thrown

down by order of the missionaries. Manoo told
me that they were monuments erected in honour
of the Indian god. Several of these ruins were
standing by the side of an old burial-place in the
edge of the woods near the shore. Each of the
graves were neatly enclosed with a wall of stone.
When we returned to the village, I was taken to
a large frame building called the missionary house,
where the missionary had prepared a roasted pig
and some tarrow, for our dinner. He designed to
entertain me after the manner of the whites, and
with this view, had placed our repast on a large
coarse table that stood in the middle of the room
with benches round it. When we were seated,
he unlocked a chest and took from it a plate
for each of us, and a knife and fork, all of which
were extremely dirty, and the knives and forks
quite covered with rust. This, however, he did
not seem to remark, although he evidently
wished me to think that he knew how to be polite, after the fashion of my country people. He
acquitted himself pretty well, to his own satisfaction, until he attempted to use the knife and fork
—but that was altogether too much for him. After making several trials in vain to cut his meat,
he asked me to assist him; and finally, before he
had half finished his dinner, laid down his clumsy
instruments and used his fingers. The chief, and
as many of the natives as could get into the room

came round us, but none of them were invited to
partake with the missionary and myself, except
Manoo, whilst the hungry crowd stood looking
wistfully at us.

Soon after we had finished our dinner, the
captain and several of the officers landed, and we
exchanged several articles with the natives for
their pigs, yams, &c. The following day was
their Sabbath and our Saturday, and they insisted
that we should remain until Monday, before any
exchange of commodities took place.   When,
however, we declared our determination to depart
that evening, they began collecting whatever
might be acceptable to us. Hogs of various
sizes, were brought to the beach in great numbers.   Needles, jack-knives, and old clothes, were
our articles of traffic, than which we could have
offered them nothing more valuable. By sun-
down, we had collected from thirty to forty hogs,
and a good supply of yams. In a few hours
more, we might have obtained twice as many
upon the same terms.

Towards the close of the day, when the missionary felt assured that it was our determination
to depart, he asked if I was a doctor, or had any
skill in medicine ; and, although I replied in the
negative, insisted upon my going to his house to
see, and prescribe for his wife, who, he told me,
was extremely ill.   Upon entering his hut, we

found her laying on a mat on the floor ; and notwithstanding the weather was oppressively warm, she was covered over with a great many pieces of the tappa cloth, head and all, and perspiring most profusely. The missionary, with great gravity, but most unceremoniously, removed all the covering, and pointed out to me her infirmity, which was nothing more than a common bile, with which she seemed to be suffering considerable pain. I declined prescribing, although repeatedly requested to do so; and at sun-down, we embarked and made sail. Had it been convenient for us to remain two days longer at Ramitarias, we could have obtained an abundant supply of whatever the island produced, for a very trifling consideration ; but although there was anchorage, it was unsheltered, and too near the shore for us to ride in safety.

At six, P. M. on the 10th of June, we took our departure from Ramitarias ; and at day-light, on the 13th, made the Island of Toubouai, bearing to the northward and eastward, about eight leagues from us. In getting in with the S. W. part of the island, we found an extensive reef, upon which the surf was breaking with great violence. We hauled round to the east side, passing two small uninhabited islands, but there was not the slightest appearance of a landing-place, the surf breaking heavily as far as we could see. At four, P. M.

we anchored on the north side, in seven fathoms
water, and sent boats in search of the harbour,
along the west shore. In the evening, they returned, having found it, and on the following
morning, we got underway, and beat up for it.
When we had advanced near the opening, through
the coral reefs that extend from the shore several
miles, a Mr. Strong, an American, came on board,
and piloted us in through a difficult passage. The
channel was narrow, and very crooked; but we
had not less than three and a half fathoms water.
Our anchorage was within a coral reef, about a
mile from the shore, in four and a half fathoms.
On the day previous to entering the harbour, we
discovered that the head of our mainmast was decayed, and badly sprung. In this situation, we
congratulated ourselves in having found a secure
harbour, where the water was tolerably smooth,
which was very essential in fixing the mast securely.

Nearly all the inhabitants of Toubouai, consisting of about two hundred, were living on the
side of the island where we were anchored, in
two different settlements. One of them was the
residence of two Otaheite missionaries, who gov-
erned in spiritual and temporal affairs; and at
the other, was the residence of the king, who,
since the coming of the missionaries, retained but
a small share of the power that formerly apper-

s

tained to his station. He lived on apparently good
terms with the missionaries, fearing their influence with the people, but secretly declaring his
aversion to them. He was the more afraid of
offending them, as there was a living example of
their displeasure constantly before him, in the
person of one who had formerly exercised the regal authority in the missionary village, of which
they had divested him for disobedience, and compelled him to live in the condition of a common
private person. Soon after the arrival of the
missionaries, the people became divided into two
parties, one of which advocated matrimony, and
the other the unrestrained indulgence which is
practised in a state of nature. The first, called
themselves the missionary party; the latter, the
party of the Tutiori. After a long struggle for
the ascendency, the Tutiories took up arms and
retired from the habitable part of the island, declaring themselves independent of the missionaries. They remained for several days undis-
turbed in their disobedience, when a party was
sent to bring them to terms. The Tutiories at
first retreated, but finally made a stand, and after
a slight show of resistance, submitted, promising
to go home and live in the observance of the missionary precepts. The dethroned king, was at
the head of the Tutiories.

At the lower village, as it was called by us,

where the king lived, was a party of our countrymen, who had been there for a number of months
building a vessel. They had completed the frame
and commenced planking, when, unfortunately, a
quarrel arose between them and the people of the
missionary village, which terminated in open hostility, and the loss of several lives. One of the
white men only, was killed. Scarcely had they
made peace with the natives, when they quar-
relled among themselves, and nearly half of their
number (four or five) discontinued their work,
and waited only for an opportunity to leave the
island. This mutinous disposition of a few, par-
alized the efforts of the whole party, and it was
probable from appearances, that the labour they
had bestowed with so much effect, would be entirely lost to themselves and their employer,
Captain Dana of Massachusetts, whom we had
seen at Oahoo.

The king and myself, became high carnies, (or
great friends) the day after our arrival; and
from that time until our departure, he did every-
thing in his power to merit my regard. My mess
was constantly supplied with bread-fruit, cocoa-
nuts, tarrow, and bananas; and whenever I was
on shore, he waited upon me everywhere with
the most friendly attention. Our friendship commenced in the following manner, simple enough,
it is true, but I believe it was not the less sincere

on that account. Seeing me with a jack-knife in my hand, he expressed a wish to look at it, when I told him that he might have it. He received it, and after observing me for a moment, put his hand upon my arm and remarked, now you and I will be high carnies. I sincerely reciprocated his kindness, so strongly recommended by the disinterested simplicity with which it was proffered. Two or three days after our arrival, I landed with a view of traversing the island. I found king Dick, as I used to call him, upon a bank of coral that stretched out from his house, with a long wooden spear in his hand, looking about in the holes for fish. He begged me to wait until he had taken one for his dinner, and he would accompany me. Accordingly, having succeeded in a few minutes afterwards, we set off together.

The island was two or three miles wide, and we had not proceeded far, when we came to an extensive marsh that runs through the middle of it. King Dick stopped, and insisted upon carrying me over on his back. Feeling that it was too menial an office to be performed by a king, although an untutored native, I remonstrated with him, and positively refused to be carried; but after resisting his importunity for some time, he took my musket in his hand, and I mounted on his shoulders. The marsh was several hundred yards wide, and king Dick found his burthen very heavy before he landed me on the opposite side. We there entered upon a romantic and extensive plain, covered with cocoa-nut, and bread-fruit trees, plantain walks, papayas, &c.; interspersed through which, were numerous huts that appeared to have been long deserted. We traversed this plain for miles, with little variation; the same pleasing prospect everywhere presenting itself, when suddenly king Dick stopped, and made the whole forest ring with the shrill notes of his voice. After repeating it for several times, he was answered at a distance, and soon afterwards, we saw a native making his approaches towards us. King Dick said something to him, and he ascended a cocoa-nut tree, after the manner of the people of the Marquesas, and threw down a sufficient quantity of nuts to quench our thirst. He afterwards conducted us to a house where there were two women and several children. They were delighted to see us, and hospitably proffered whatever they had of refreshment. They gave us a preparation of dried bread-fruit, of which king Dick ate very heartily, but to me it was scarcely palatable. Near the house there were several citron and lemon trees, the only ones that I saw on the island.

In our route back, we met with large quantities of sugar cane in a wild state. We passed the burial-place of the village, where, beside two or

three newly made graves, were rudely carved
images placed there in conformity to a native
custom, that had not yet been abolished by the
influence of the missionaries.   When we arrived
at king Dick's house, we found dinner waiting for
us.   It consisted of the fish he had taken in
the morning before our departure, roasted fowls,
bread-fruit, tarrow, &c.   The whole was wrapped up in plantain leaves, and placed on a mat
upon the floor, around which, we all seated
ourselves, there being a number of visiters present.   During our repast, king Dick went frequently to a large chest, where he kept a bottle
of rum I had given him, and, after proffering me
the bottle, he would help himself, and lock it up
in the chest again, without taking the least notice
of the rest of his visiters.   No miser ever guarded his treasure more penuriously than the king
did his bottle of rum; not only on this, but all
other occasions.   His house was large, and a
lounging place for all the idle people of his village; and, although there were always a number
present when I made my visits, and he never
failed to offer me a portion of his favourite bever-
age, the wistful lookers-on received not the slightest notice.   I once ventured to propose to him to
give some to his friends, but he said no, it was
too good for them.   When, after a week's stay at
Toubouai, our departure was spoken of, king

Dick expressed the liveliest regret, and proposed
going with us.   We told him that he would never
be able to get back again; to which he replied,
that he should not care about returning.   The
day before we left, he sent me, on board, an
abundant sea-stock, of fruits and vegetables, and
a good-sized hog.   As a parting gift, I dressed
him up in an old uniform of mine, that seemed to
give him infinite pleasure.   To his presents, his
wife added several pieces of the tappa cloth, some
of which, were as fine specimens of the native
manufacture, as I ever met with anywhere.

At Toubouai, we added considerably to our
collection of curiosities.   The most ingeniously
wrought article, was a lash, used by the natives
for brushing the flies off of their backs.   The
handles were carved to represent a man's face,
or some animal familiar to them.   The lash
itself, was, in several strands, finely braided from
twine of the cocoa-nut husk.   The natives were,
in general, naked, except a wrapper round their
waists, and had a sickly and feeble look.   The
island is very fertile, producing, in many parts,
large quantities of cocoa-nut and bread-fruit, and
is capable, without further improvement, of sustaining some thousands of people.   The population has greatly diminished within the recollection
of recent visiters.   It must have been much greater when visited by the mutineers of the Bounty,

who built a fort on the island, but afterwards became dissatisfied, and left it in consequence of the
treacherous and hostile character of the natives.
The only survivor of those guilty men, who is
now the patriarch of Pitcairn's Island, states,
that they had war with the natives previous to
leaving Toubouai, and that they killed a great
many of them. His estimate of the inhabitants
at that time, is fifteen thousand. King Dick told
me, that the huts we saw on the side of the island
opposite to where we anchored, were once inhabited by people who were all dead. We obtained wood and water of a good quality, without
much labour. Hogs were scarce, and we got
none but what were presented to us. The natives
gave us a few domestic fowls, in exchange for
writing paper. The paper was used by the women for making paste-board for a bonnet, that
had just been introduced amongst them by the
wives of the Otaheite missionaries.

On the island of Toubouai, there is a tree, the
bark of which, makes excellent cordage. It is
produced in great abundance, and grows to the
size of six or eight inches in diameter. After
the ship builders were interrupted in their work,
by the discontent of some of the party, the remainder made a rope-walk, and devoted themselves to making rope of this bark. They
had several small cables, and a considerable

quantity of rope. We purchased some, and found it to wear nearly, or quite, as well as hemp. Arrow root, grows spontaneously upon the island, and has been taken away by several vessels, as an article of commerce. We were informed that the scarcity of hogs was in consequence of a great many having been carried off recently, by a vessel belonging to the missionaries. Also, that they lay all the small islands under contribution, and annually send their small vessels to collect the hogs, which they barrel, and send to Port Jackson. This may be true or not. It was positively asserted.

Our stock of bread was nearly exhausted, and what remained, was in a damaged state. Having failed in all our attempts to obtain a supply of yams, that would enable us to reach the coast of South America, an examination was held upon the bread, to the end, that we might adopt such expedients as should be deemed most proper. Valparaiso, was our most direct port; there was but one inhabited island (Oparro,) in our way, and that at some distance from a straight course. To avoid, however, so disagreeable a circumstance as being without bread, we determined to touch at Oparro, and get whatever we could for a substitute. Accordingly, we put to sea on the 22d of June, and on the 25th, made Oparro, a little before day-light, five leagues from us.

When we came near, its appearance was rude
and inhospitable in the extreme, being a mass of
rugged mountains, about a thousand feet high,
and eight or ten miles in circumference. On the
north-west side, there were no signs of inhabitants.
The mountains rose almost perpendicularly from
the Ocean, and we sounded frequently, close to
the shore, without getting bottom. In rounding
the island, to the northward and eastward, we
opened a valley, where there was a number of
huts, and some patches of tarrow. A boat was
sent in shore, and two of the natives came on
board, who informed us that there was a harbour
to the eastward. We continued on, and after landing at one or two other small valleys, where there
were huts and tarrow patches, opened a beautiful
deep bay, that had an appearance of great fertility. Soon afterwards, an Englishman came on
board, and offered to pilot us in. He had not
advanced far with the vessel, before she grounded
on a bank of coral, but fell off immediately, on
putting the helm down and throwing all aback.
We were everywhere surrounded by shoals of
coral, and fearful of accidents, came to outside of
the harbour, where we had ten fathoms of water
on one side, and five on the other. The boats
were sent off immediately, in search of tarrow.
It was planted everywhere, in large patches,
where there was a small valley, through which

a stream of water found its way from the mountains to the sea, and at a distance, the hills were green with another species we had not before seen, called mountain tarrow. The latter is superior to the low land tarrow, and will keep longer at sea.

When we landed in the bay, which was several miles deep, we found two different missionary establishments, occupied by natives of Otaheite. No one else, that we saw, seemed to have any authority. They permitted us to dig as much tarrow as we pleased, without asking any return for it, and by night, we had as much on board as we knew what to do with. One of the missionary establishments was situated at the extreme depth of the bay. On landing there, I was met by the missionaries themselves, and conducted to their house, where their wives, who were also from Otaheite, received me, dressed in their own island costume, with large straw bonnets on their heads. After remaining with them for a few minutes, I repaired to the place where the boats' crew were employed in collecting tarrow. A group of natives, male and female, had assembled round, none of whom, could be prevailed upon by the rewards we offered them, to assist our people in their occupation. They had a sickly look, almost without an exception. Their dress differed altogether from any we had before seen. It consisted of a heavy mat of grass, weighing from ten to fifteen pounds, which was thrown over their shoulders, and another light mat of the same material, for the loins. Their deportment was modest and retiring, and they evinced a disposition to have but little intercourse with us. A few of their houses were scattered about upon the hills. They were extremely miserable, and might, without disparagement, be compared to dog kennels. They were long, and very narrow, and about three or four feet high, so that when one entered them, it was necessary to get down upon the hands and knees. The Otaheite missionaries were distinguished from the natives, by wearing the tappa cloth, of their own island, and an old cloth jacket they had obtained from white visiters. I added something to their stock of clothes, before I took leave of them, for which, they gave me many thanks. When I returned on board, I found the other two missionaries there, and several of the natives, who had accompanied the captain. They spent the night with us, and the next morning, showed us where to obtain a quantity of the mountain tarrow. It is large, and very much resembles the West India yam. For a vessel long at sea, and requiring vegetables, there is none more valuable.

The Englishman who came on board to act as our pilot, was residing at the island, in charge of

a party which had been left there by the English
Consul at the Sandwich Islands, to collect beach
la mer, a valuable article of commerce, at Canton.
The collecting of sandal-wood, was also to be an
object of their attention ; but they told us, that
both were scarce, and difficult to obtain—a statement, we considered, of doubtful veracity.

At 2, P. M., on the 27th of June, we got underway, and made sail for Valparaiso, which is distant from Oparro, about three thousand five hundred miles.   This island, which is called by the
discoverer, Oparro, is called by the natives, Lapa.
It is situated in latitude 27 degrees 34 minutes
south, west longitude 144 degrees.   At 5, P. M.,
we saw the islands, called by Quiros, Los Corones, and hauled up, until eight, to clear them.

For the first three days after we sailed, it blew
a severe gale from the westward, after which, it
became more moderate, but nearly all our passage to Valparaiso, was wet and boisterous.   It
was less disagreeable, however, than we anticipated, as the wind was almost constantly fair.
We had the more reason to apprehend a severe
trial of our fortitude, as it was in the dead of winter that we were advancing into a high latitude,
after having been a long time within the tropics,
and besides that, our sails and rigging were very
much worn, some of our articles of provisions
were quite exhausted, and others, of the first ne-

cessity, reduced to a small quantity. If, therefore, we had encountered tedious gales ahead, we
must have suffered greatly in our shattered and
ill-fitted condition.

At 4, P. M., on the 19th of July, we made the
island of Mas a Fuera, on the coast of Chili,
seventy miles from us, and at midnight, passed
close to it. At day-light, Juan Fernandes, was
in sight, fifty miles off. We passed it a little
after meridian. It is very mountainous, but well
covered with trees. The interesting fable of
Robinson Crusoe's adventures, has given it a lasting fame, and rendered it an object of curiosity to
all who visit this part of the Pacific Ocean. It is
very fertile, and has been tolerably well cultivated. The Spanish captain-general of Chili,
formerly made it a place of banishment, and after
the revolution took place in that country, it was
appropriated to the same purpose, by the patriots
and royalists, as they alternately came into power. A considerable town was built by the exiles,
who were sent there at different times, and the finest
fruits of Chili are produced in great abundance.
The cattle that have been left upon the island,
are running wild in large herds, and several persons have found it profitable to send parties
there to kill them for their hides. The island
produces some sandal-wood, but it is small, and
has never been collected in large quantities.

Fish, that very much resemble our codfish, and a variety of other kinds are taken in the greatest abundance around Juan Fernandez and Mas a Fuera.   It is believed that if a fishery were established there by some of our enterprising countrymen, it would be found a source of great emolument.   The privileges that might be considered necessary for the prosperity of a company formed with this object, could easily be obtained from the government of Chili, and there is no apparent cause why the most successful results should not be realized.   It seems only necessary to call the attention of our capitalists to this subject, to have all its advantages secured to our country.   It has a fine harbour for the prevailing winds of summer, but in the winter season, when the winds set in from the northward, it is exposed.   It lies a little more than three hundred miles from the coast of Chili, and in the summer months I have known open boats to pass between it and Valparaiso.

On the 23d of July, we anchored in the harbour of Valparaiso, a little before day-light, to the gratification of our friends, who were becoming very much alarmed for our safety, no information of us having been received during the whole period of our absence.   Thus, in a vessel of 180 tons burthen, poorly fitted, and having on board only about four months' provisions, when we sailed from the coast of Peru, we performed a cruise of upwards of eleven months in an unfrequented Ocean, rendering to our countrymen, and many of the people whom we visited, important benefits, besides realizing the most successful results in the primary object of our cruise. Its beneficial effects will long be felt by our countrymen, who are engaged in the whale-fishery; and, although we suffered many hardships, privations, and dangers, we were happy in being the instruments, in the hands of Providence and our government, of proving that crime cannot go unpunished in the remotest part of the earth, and that no situation is so perilous as to justify despair.

Paulding, Hiram, 1797–1878.

 Journal of a cruise of the United States schooner Dolphin among the islands of the Pacific Ocean and a visit to the Mulgrave Islands, in pursuit of the mutineers of the whale ship Globe ... With a new introd. by A. Grove Day. Honolulu, University of Hawaii Press, 1970 [°1831]

 xxi, 258 p. map (on lining paper), port. 16 cm. $6.00

  1. Oceanica—Description and travel.   i. Title.   ii. Title: Cruise of the United States schooner Dolphin.

DU21.P32 1970b   919   77-119793
ISBN 0-87022-616-9   MARC

Library of Congress   71 [4]